Fly Fishing in Ireland

Fly Fishing in Ireland

JOHN BAILEY

GILL & MACMILLAN

Published in Ireland by
Gill & Macmillan Ltd
Hume Avenue, Park West, Dublin 12
with associated companies throughout the world
www.gillmacmillan.ie

© John Bailey 2003

0 7171 3420 2

Designed by Andrew Easton
Edited by Ian Whitelaw
Printed in Malaysia

This book is typeset in Caxton Light 10pt on 17pt.

*The paper used in this book comes from the wood pulp of managed forests.
For every tree felled, at least one tree is planted,
thereby renewing natural resources.*

All rights reserved.
No part of this publication may be copied, reproduced or transmitted
in any form or by any means, without permission of the publishers.

A CIP catalogue record for this book is available
from the British Library.

1 3 5 4 2

Spring 10

MIGHTY LOUGH CORRIB
The Grandeur of Ashford
Castle 12

LOUGH ARROW
Arrow Lodge and
the Duck Fly 20

LOUGH INAGH
The Old and the New 28

BALLYNAHINCH
Castle, River,
and Lough 36

CARAGH AND CLOON
Glencar House Hotel 44

THE ART OF DAPPING
Mayfly Magic 52

Summer 54

THE CORK BLACKWATER
Blackwater Lodge 56

LOST LIMERICK
Mulcair and Shannon 62

LOUGH CURRANE
The Sea Trout of Kerry 72

THE KERRY BLACKWATER
The Perfect Spate River 80

BUNDORRAGHA RIVER
Restoring the
Delphi Fishery 88

THE WESTERN LOUGHS
Corrib and Mask
in Summer 96

TOTAL FLY FISHING
Casting for
Alternatives 102

Autumn 106

**RETURN TO
ARROW LODGE**
A Piker's Paradise 108

**A RIVER RUNS
THROUGH IT**
Towns on the Water 114

**LOUGHS CONN
AND CULLIN**
Healy's Hotel 120

MELVIN AND THE ERNE
Sonaghan, Gillaroo,
and Sea Trout 128

A MODEL FISHERY
The Lessons
of Ballinlough 136

THE MIDLAND LOUGHS
The Tale of
Lough Sheelin 142

Winter 148

WINTER ON THE WATER
Time for Reflection 150

INDEX 158
ACKNOWLEDGEMENTS 160

Introduction

"Make the most of Ireland. It's there waiting for you, and you should enjoy every splendid second of the fishing and the fun that it has to offer."

Thank you to the people of Ireland. The records that I've kept assiduously since childhood reveal that I've fished in 46 countries, but nowhere have I met folk who are more fun, more welcoming, or more full of information than the Irish. For me, the year 2002 was spent very largely in Ireland, touring and talking fishing. Not a bad job you'd say, and you'd be right: I thought I already knew Ireland, but to get to the bones of any country you need to spend solid months there.

And now, even though I've done that, I'm still horribly aware that there's much that I will have missed. There can be no other country in the world with quite as much water per square mile as Ireland possesses. Perhaps that's why fishing is so important to the psyche of the nation. It doesn't matter how small the village, whether you're in a shop or a bar, whether you're talking to a man or a woman, old or young, everyone has a fishing tale to tell. A monster old pike perhaps, or a fabulous trout, or a salmon the size of a suckling pig… in Ireland everything is possible, it seems.

Around a century ago, Augustus Grimble wrote a very stern account of the state of Irish rivers. I'm sure that if we are ever to meet up in the loughs of heaven he'll put me in no doubt that this particular guide is frivolous in the extreme, and that too much of it relies on fantasy, philosophy, and photography. Perhaps he'll be right, but I have tried not to be too blinded by Ireland's evident and seductive charms. As in any country in the world, I've tried to see both the good and the bad. For example, one of the beauties of Irish fishing is surely the fact there are so few commercial venues. Ireland is truly a country of wild fish and, where these are in danger, far-sighted fishery owners are working hard to help them. Irish fishing faces a huge threat from fish farms and their attendant clouds of sea lice. There are also almost certainly too many farm animals in Ireland, and water enrichment has proved to be a massive problem on many loughs that aren't set in completely barren landscapes. Forestation hasn't always helped, nor has the pressure on fisheries from ever-growing numbers of anglers and the predations of a lingering class of poachers.

Ireland hasn't totally escaped the pressures of the modern world, and you mustn't visit Ireland thinking it's some sort of earthly Paradise, a lost Utopia, but you have your own part to play in a praiseworthy struggle to both maintain and improve the fly fishing, which is probably the best in Europe today. As you'll see during the course of this book, Ireland is full of anglers with intelligence and bravery, committed to improving the state of what are often still very good fisheries indeed. Innumerable men, such as Ken Whelan, James Pembroke, and Patrick O'Flaherty, are fighting courageously for the future of Irish fishing. This is partly for economic reasons, of course, but it's done largely out of love.

Poaching has always been a huge problem in Ireland, but this seems to be now on the wane, partly due to education, partly because it's no longer a necessity, nor any more seen as a declaration of independence against absentee landlords. Communities are beginning to see poachers as plunderers of a common source of wealth. Strip the river of its salmon and you are denying a livelihood to all those that work in the tourist trade at every level. Education has also led to a growing trend for catch-and-release. River management has improved. Most of the nets have been bought off the estuaries. It's all but illegal now to sell any wild fish for profit. It is illegal to sell wild salmon as I write, and as you read it may already be the case with trout as well.

RING OF BRIGHT WATER *Sunset, and waterfowl search for the food that has fallen onto the water's surface during the course of the day. This is also when a big, wild trout can be especially vulnerable as it cruises for its supper in the surface film in the last of the light.*

With the weather on your side, you can come to Ireland hopeful of some superb fishing. Whatever the conditions, you will see the most wondrous of scenery: the west coast in particular takes my own breath away no matter how many times I visit it. As I've already said, the people will make you welcome everywhere. It will be impossible for you not to make friends with the guides who accompany you. Enjoy the bars and the banter, and you will come to realize that there is a true Irish experience to be discovered.

Richard Keays brought this home to me one summer's day when we were walking a delightful river near to his guesthouse. He told me of an American banker who had visited him year upon year upon year. He always caught fish, but increasingly he enjoyed simply walking and watching the different waters.

In the summer of 2001, the American happened to be at Richard's, along with some Frenchmen. The waters were low and clear, and everyone was struggling. The Frenchmen were vociferous in their complaints. On the fourth or fifth night, after another troublesome dinner, the American could listen no longer, and he put the French completely straight upon the philosophy of fishing. "Don't you realize what a privilege it is to fish waters like this with people like these?" he said. "I have fished all over America and throughout most of Europe, and I can tell you that this is precious and special and unique. To waste your time here is to fritter away your entire lives. Just

A FEROCIOUS BEAUTY *The author admires a sleekly handsome ferox trout. The ferox is no ill-conditioned, large-headed predator, but a sub-species with enormous power and beauty.*

look around you and seize the beauty that is everywhere." Richard's American worked at the World Trade Centre. Christmas 2001 came around, and for the first time in 10 years, sadly, no Christmas card with a New York postal code arrived through the Keays' letterbox.

Make the most of Ireland. It's there waiting for you, and you should enjoy every splendid second of the fishing and the fun that it has to offer.

Spring

"Spring in Ireland is one of the big fly-fishing experiences, and it's just got to be tried."

You're on your way to Ireland at the start of the fishing year, and your thoughts are zinging with excitement. You know that you're going to find boats that are freshly painted, their outboard engines just raring to go. The fish will be rested, so you know that you can expect titanic struggles, and won't the scream of the reel be that much sweeter after your four or five months' lay off? You've probably brought a new bit of kit to try out – something from a winter catalogue that you fondly pored over through the dark, cold months.

Yes, you've got all this to look forward to, but you can be pretty sure that you're going to meet up with some foul weather, too. This is Ireland, perched on the lip of the Atlantic, so be prepared for the storms that, at some stage, will gallop your way. If you're warm and dry, you'll fish well: if you're cold and miserable, the Guinness will simply draw you in early to sit at the bar with no tale to tell.

You should never be in too much of a hurry to give in on a spring day, even if the weather is foul. At some stage, you'll be rewarded for sticking it out. There's almost always going to be a moment when the setting sun sinks beneath the clouds and, even if only briefly, you'll be treated to the most extraordinary of nature's light shows. At that point of sunset, there's always a chance that the wind will slacken and give you just half an hour of glorious fishing. The lough that has been wild and furious all day long can suddenly become still – the air warms, insects hatch, and the trout, evidently starving, begin to somersault. A miserable day has become a miracle one. Ireland can certainly be tough in the spring and the rewards are hard won, but they can be spine-tingling.

If the open water is truly too wild for all but the insane, think laterally. Almost anywhere in Ireland there are bound to be small streams close by, often sheltered, frequently overlooked, and almost always fishable if you ask the local farmer. The trout might not be a pound or even half that, but who cares when they're beautiful, spirited, and hard-fighting? As Christopher Yates once wrote, "I suppose a perfect angling day has got to have a fish in it somewhere, but the ingredients for perfection don't necessarily have to include a big one, nor do they have to contain moments of fanfare and alleluia."

Mind you, at any time in spring, the sudden promise of summer can shimmer. A cuckoo calling, a break in the cloud and 20 minutes of beating sunshine, the splosh of a silver salmon, or word of an early sea trout all mean that kinder days are close at hand. This is the time, too, for the glorious mayfly, and nowhere will you see them in such splendid, light-dazzling profusion as you will in the west of Ireland.

If you're a real play-it-safe merchant, you'll probably save your trip for June, perhaps the most reliable of all months, but you'll be missing out on so much. Spring in Ireland is one of the big fly-fishing experiences, and it's just got to be tried.

MIGHTY LOUGH CORRIB
The Grandeur of Ashford Castle

"... here is a whole class of men whose lives have been made so much less ordinary by their involvement in angling."

If Ireland is important to us as anglers, then we in turn are equally important to Ireland. On a crucial, economic level, the airline and ferry companies, any number of car hire firms, and an absolute plethora of hotels, guesthouses, and bed and breakfast establishments rely heavily on the patronage of the world angler, as well as on Irish nationals. Fishing has been big business in Ireland for decades, but it's more than just a matter of Euros: you only have to travel a few score miles and see the number of bars rejoicing in piscatorial soubriquets – of which the Fisherman's Rest is a favourite – to realize just how deeply rooted angling is in the country's psyche.

In the lives of individuals, angling runs deeper still. Talk to the Irish guides both past and present – and there are many, many of them – and you'll realize that here is a whole class of men whose lives have been made so much less ordinary by their involvement in angling. Jimmy Foy, for example, has guided on Lough Corrib for 60 years or more, principally from that grandest of bases, Ashford Castle, and his life has been given a sparkle that he could never have achieved from a tractor seat.

Should I talk first of Corrib or of the Castle? I suppose, as this is a fishing book, the lough must come first. It's the largest water in the Republic, 40 miles long and 9 miles across from Cong to Oughterard. Its deepest point is 152 feet and it averages 30 to 40 feet in depth. The lough boasts 365 islands, of which 10 are inhabited, the most populous being home to 15 families. Corrib has been a spiritual magnet throughout the ages: on the islands and the shores there are the remains of monasteries, churches, and burial stones, many dating back 1,500 years or more. It is a beautiful water, sheltering in the lee of the Maumturk Mountains at the toe of Ireland's Joyce

THE MYSTERIOUS CORRIB *There's a glorious freedom about Lough Corrib, so vast, so smiling with limitless potential. A whiff of sunshine and it's a bounteous, joyful place: come the cloud and the mist, and mystery settles upon it like a shroud.*

ARCHITECTURAL MAGNIFICENCE *In the gloom of a spring evening, Ashford Castle looms over the lough. This fabulous creation is fittingly exotic for such an awesome water.*

DAWN SPLENDOUR *There really is no better time to be out on the water than when the mists of dawn are rising. Fish are often feeding hard in the surface film, so look for them in bays and moving up feeder streams.*

LIGHT ON THE LOUGH *The western loughs are marvels of constantly shifting light. It doesn't matter how dour the day, there'll always come a point, generally around sunset, when the whole scene suddenly explodes into life.*

country. As a wild, brown trout fishery, it's very doubtful whether any water in Europe surpasses it. Certainly it holds good salmon, perch, roach, pike, and eels, but the brown trout is the absolute star of Lough Corrib.

Along with the Castle. View Ashford Castle on a windy, rain-swept night and it looks as though it has stepped from the hell of Macbeth. See it across the lake first thing on a morning in mid summer when the mist is rising, and the sight is enough to eclipse our finest visions of Camelot. Approach it from the water at dusk after a day's fishing, when the lights are on and perhaps a piano is tinkling out across the lawns, and it looks like a great ocean liner, or a magical citadel of the gods.

Fond Memories

I was taken to meet Jimmy Foy by Frank Costello, the young fishery manager at Ashford, and I was warned that Jimmy could be reticent, that he might need a little coaxing. It was a bleak day, with the rain coursing down the windows of his trim cottage, but it wasn't long before images of Jimmy's life with Corrib began to bubble up like the waters of his lough itself. It all began in childhood, fishing with ash or hazel poles cut from the forest, stripped of their bark and whipped up with a line. If ever he or one of his friends hooked a salmon on the troll with gear like this, it was simply a matter of throwing the pole overboard (and quickly!) and waiting for the fish to tire itself out against the buoyancy of the wood. And sometimes it worked.

Jimmy spoke of mayfly hatches so dense that you could barely see your hand in front of your face, of huge storms on the lough when the boatmen were forced to bivouac for the night on any island that would give them sanctuary, and he told of some of the many anglers who have shared his knowledge over the years.

"At first, after the war, it was mostly the Irish anglers coming over from Dublin, but very soon the English began to follow, and in those days we had our regulars who came year after year and stayed for two weeks minimum. We got to know them as friends. Mr Dobson, for example, fished with me for the browns, the sea trout, and the salmon for 32 years. He always had a Jaguar, and even though he changed it every couple of years, it would always have the same registration… yes, RPD 99. He used to smoke a pipe as he drove, and Mrs Dobson would shake out and fill a new one so that there was never one out of his mouth. What Mr Dobson realized, as many gentlemen did in those days, was that Corrib cannot be rushed. It can be dead and more dead, and then suddenly spark into life. He put up with the slow days because he knew that there'd be good to follow. That's why he kept coming back – he understood the place."

We pause for another cup of Mrs Foy's excellent tea and she shows me photographs of the Dobsons, of her own daughter's wedding, and of the grandchildren that followed. All neatly framed. Not a speck of dust.

"The people with money in those days seemed to have more leisure than they do now. It's just no use coming to Corrib for two days, because you might not see a fish. I remember one time when the lake was off that cost me dearly. I had a Scotsman with me and all he wanted was a big trout. He told me he'd give me a pound in money for every pound the trout was in weight. For four days we trolled, and on the very last day he hooked a big one. It really was a good fish and I could feel the money in my pocket. But, of course, it came off and away he went cursing, and me not a jot the better off. I'd still got plenty of bait, and so the next day I decided to have a little fish for myself. First one – seven and a half pounds. Fixed up the bait again, rowed 200 yards – five and a half pounds. Had my lunch, cast out, and there was a three pounder. Believe me, money was very short in those days and couldn't I have done with that £16!

"Over the years, I've ghillied for thousands of anglers from all nations, and I've liked them nearly all. The Americans can be very good fly fishers once they're used to still water, and some of the English can be excellent, brought up as they are on reservoirs. I've even had one or two Russians, and when you do get one you never forget him. I remember one burly chap from Moscow who came over in September, probably the best time for salmon on the lough. We trolled for some days and then got stuck into a huge fish. My Russian man wasn't playing him well at all and let him get into a weed bed. I managed to manoeuvre him free, and the fish simply got into the

"Over the years, I've ghillied for thousands of anglers from all nations, and I've liked them nearly all."

MASTERS OF CORRIB *Jimmy Foy (right) and Frank Costello stand under Jimmy's largest Corrib trout. Between them, there's little that these men don't know about the lough.*

WHITE LIGHTNING *An old misconception about ferox still maintains that they are lean, ill-conditioned fish that don't fight. Far from true, believe me. A ferox will fight until your eyes pop and your shoulders ache.*

MINNOWS

The brickeen, the minnows from the mountain streams around the lough, form a very important part of the diet in Lough Corrib. During the winter floods, these minnows get washed into the lake and the trout go mad for them. Old stagers used to catch them in the hills in brandy bottles, mount them, and troll them in the lough with great success. However, artificials are now available – try minkies around the rocks for some palpitating early season sport.

next one. Against all my protests, the Russian just heaved and heaved and the line broke, and so by God did his temper. He stood in the boat there trembling and swearing and raging at the heavens and at me. We nearly had a stand-up fight in the boat, him swearing it was my fault and me telling him it was his.

"Only one other man sticks in my mind for all the wrong reasons. He was a military man and as bossy and mean as anybody I've ever come across. I'd got him hooked into a big trout, but during the fight he stopped concentrating altogether, just asking me, 'Jimmy, which will be the cheapest way to send this home to the taxidermist… boat… train… air…?' Anyway, the fish – and it really was a monster – broke free. I looked at him and told him that the fish had found the cheapest way! Just like that big Russian, he flew into a wild temper and blamed his tackle, me, the fish, everybody but himself. In the end, he began to sulk and asked to be left to fish on his own for a while on one of the islands. Well, I dropped him off and made my way back to the Castle. It was almost nightfall when he managed to attract another boatman's attention and get himself back home. I was worried all right and came straight to Frank's father, the fishery manager himself in those days, to try and excuse myself. 'Don't worry Jimmy,' he told me. 'He's been upsetting the whole Castle and nobody will say a word against you!'

"Just about the time I started on the lough we were given outboard motors, but it was around the war years and there was never any petrol for them. So most of the time we'd row, and that meant – on a lake that's 68 square miles in extent – we boatmen kept to our own patches. Nowadays, with the huge engines modern anglers have got, there's a temptation to rip-roar here, there, and everywhere. My own view is that it's better to stay put and get to know an area intimately. When you're powering around the place you not only disturb the water itself but you can miss patches simply by travelling so much. Take your time, and you'll get to know Corrib a lot better."

THE FASCINATION OF FEROX

Frank drove me back to the Castle. Corrib was always there over the fields, a great looming grey presence in the mist. "Things have changed since Jimmy and my father's day," said Frank. "But then Corrib, like all waters, changes constantly anyway. At the moment we're seeing it as hugely productive, and the brown trout fishing has possibly never been better, despite the explosion of roach stocks. In fact, the roach may have done us good in one way. There have never been so many and such big ferox trout in the lough. I had my own monster just last year. To be truthful, I was after pike at the time, positioned behind an island using a dead roach as bait, when the line ran out. It wasn't until it sploshed and I saw it that I realized it was a huge trout. I've never seen a more beautiful one either. Fabulously marked. Amazing condition. And, of course, its weight – 25 pounds and an exact yard long – the largest caught in Ireland since 1894 and the biggest ever from Corrib. It's not alone in the lough. There may be others bigger yet. You know, my father fished all his life and never got one of over 12 pounds, so perhaps the roach are doing us a good turn."

Ferox! Well, I can tell you, my own eyes light up at the word. There is not a more glamorous, dashing, exotic fish that swims anywhere, not just in Ireland. My own feroxing career has focused largely on northwest Scotland and has been as tough as they come: remote lochs; snowstorms to blanket out the shores; gales strong enough to raise spindrift columns thick as armies; damp, cold nights in far-flung bothies; shipwreck! And very, very few fish indeed. Scotland just does not have the density of fish that Corrib boasts. Had I put the thousands of hours spent on those Scottish vastnesses into fishing Corrib... well, I can't imagine what I would have caught.

Some anglers regard trolling as a boring way of fishing, without art or excitement, and, even as a keen and practised troller myself, I admit there is something mechanical about it. Nonetheless, even if it will never bewitch to the same degree as the fly, there's a lot more to it than meets the purist's eye. The fact that Frank and other master fly anglers – such as Basil Shiels, further around the lough – spend time trolling speaks volumes: ferox are worth any game whatsoever. They are sheer magnificence, and just to see one makes you gasp.

Frank recommends trolling with a natural roach, and fish of six to eight inches are generally easily caught. Failing a dead bait, a Rapala Super Shad is a proven alternative, especially in the colours silver, silver roach, and green-gold roach. Troll carefully and relatively slowly, Frank says. Cover islands with deep drop-offs and any other interesting underwater contours. The classic time is a fine summer's evening after a warm day as the sun goes down.

According to Frank, an 11-foot rod is about right, allied with 15-pound line. A fixed spool reel or multiplier is ideal. Always use a wire trace, in case you hook a pike. If you're using a natural bait, make sure that you have enough lead to get the bait down at least 10 or 15 feet, but put on too much and you'll begin to hit bottom.

A GOLDEN AGE *Old photographs always have a nostalgia about them, but in the present age, fishing records like this serve to remind us that the sport has a long and cherished history. Fishing has always been enjoyed by people of all ages and both sexes.*

The Grandeur of Ashford Castle

THE CORRIB CALENDAR

The Corrib season opens very early in the spring, on February 15th in fact. The fish are generally hard on the bottom, feeding on shrimp, snails, and caddis, but you'll often find the fish in shallow water even at this early time of the year. The weather this early can be a major problem to both the angler and the fish. Sometimes it's hard to get out on the water, and when you do you will find the fish in poorish condition.

For most anglers, spring fishing begins around March 20th when you see the first fly hatch, the duck fly, better known in England as buzzers. On Corrib, as on many Irish loughs, the ducks go absolutely mad for them, and hence the name. Duck fly fishing has really taken off in Ireland over the last few years and many Irish fishermen themselves have started using epoxy imitations with devastating results. Concentrate over the deep holes that have a bottom of weed and mud. You'll find trout concentrated there, picking off the flies on their way from the bottom to the surface.

The duck fly struggles on well into April, but around the 16th of the month the olives begin to appear on the lough. Once these have started to hatch, the trout gradually switch onto them. Concentrate your olive fishing over weeded areas. The fish will come onto the surface and feed hard. Use nymphs in flat, bright conditions and wets or dries if it's blowy, but don't forget the buzzer, even though the olives are about. In fact, April can often be class fishing with big trout on the buzzer.

The olives stagger into the start of the mayfly fishing season. The appearance of the mayfly depends on weather but they begin to appear between May 12th and 15th and keep on going until the beginning of June. The longer the mayfly hatch drags on, the more the fish get sick of them. Of course, dapping with mayfly (see page 52) is an art in its own right, accounting for some seriously big fish at this time of the year. What's often overlooked is that you can catch grilse on mayfly as well. This can be fascinating fishing in May and June when the fish are fresh in. In fact, with just a little encouragement, grilse fishing could become a major part of the sport on Corrib.

If Frank Costello himself has any favourite style of fishing it is probably using the dry buzzer in the evening when the lake's surface can really begin to boil. Very big fish can come up at any time between 9 and 10pm, but in late May, as the nights are really getting bright, the best time can be two o'clock in the morning. Indeed, as Frank says, the best time to go out is when the rest are coming in. Few boats are out at this time of night and it's as though most anglers are afraid of the lake or just think that fishing so late is a waste of time, but quality fish of up to five pounds are common in the near-blackness. You are, of course, fishing by feel and sound, investigating the surface film of the lough. You can either move the buzzers yourself or just leave them skating in any surface breeze that there may be. Don't make the mistake of using too light a leader: there are big fish about. Eight to ten pound breaking strain at the point is about right. In the darkness the line is much less visible, and these big fish hit buzzers like dynamite, so be prepared.

THE FOOD ITEMS

HOUSE OF GRAVEL
Caddis larvae construct their cases out of all sorts of material – generally weed, pebbles, or sand.

THE HATCHED INSECT
The larva lives for a year and then, after pupating within the case, it breaks free and emerges as a winged adult sedge.

MINI LOBSTER
Crayfish are the refuse collectors of the riverbed. Small crayfish, and larger dead ones, are often targeted by trout.

FRESHWATER SNAILS
All snails need a good supply of calcium to build their shells, and the rich waters of the Irish west provide an ideal habitat.

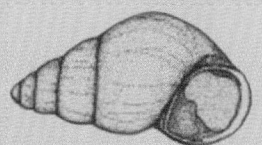

Frank stresses the importance of making sure you've got your boat routine sorted out. Once you get a take, reel in the other rods and take stock of the wind. If you're out in the open and there's no danger in drifting, knock off the engine. If you're going to drift into an island or onto rocks, keep the engine in neutral and watch carefully for any approaching hazards. Play the fish lightly and don't be overly hard on them. Hook holds are often light and ferox are manic head shakers. Fish are generally landed from the boat because of the difficulty of beaching on most of the islands, especially in a wind. For this reason, place an unhooking mat or something similarly soft in the bottom of the boat so that the ferox isn't injured.

I wouldn't disagree with any of this: how could I, considering how many ferox Frank has taken? And yet, ferox fishing is not an exact science. My own experiences suggest that there are many questions still to be answered. Are the Corrib ferox really bigger now than in the past, or is gear better and are more people trying for them? Should you troll slowly, or does speed give ferox less time to examine lures? Is there any point targeting fish when research in Scotland and Europe suggests that many ferox keep on the move, drifting with the currents until their paths cross a wandering char shoal? Perhaps you should just troll and troll until you hit lucky? And how big can ferox, in truth, grow? If the 39-pound Loch Awe fish taken a century ago is to be believed, then Corrib still has a way to go. But what if it gets there? What if ferox have the genetic capability to exceed 40 pounds and what if the roach can fuel this? What will trolling for fish such as these be like?

Frank drops me off by the Castle, but I don't care to go in immediately and so I walk to the water's edge where the rain continues to dapple the surface. I look about me, awed by the beauty, by the history, and by the sheer bounteous immensity of it all. This is a magical place inhabited by special men and special creatures. Jimmy's last words come back to me. I can see him clearly, leaning forward, holding me with his gaze. "But let me tell you one thing. I've been out many, many times in my life with famous men and politicians and multi-multi millionaires. And I've listened to them and I've watched them and I've thought about their lives. And there's never been a single, solitary second when I've envied a-one of them. There hasn't been a day in my life when I haven't got up longing for my work to begin – and there's not many of them can say that."

"There hasn't been a day in my life when I haven't got up longing for my work to begin..."

LOUGH ARROW
Arrow Lodge and the Duck Fly

It is the evening of April 9th, after a blue, warm day, and I'm in a living miracle. April is, as Rob Maloney says, the sunset month here in Ireland, so let's forget the fishing for a while and watch the light play over the landscape, over the waters of Lough Arrow, and let's soak up the immensity of history and feel the pulse of the past. From where Rob and I sit in his boat, rocking over 10 feet of water, the sun is burning up in the west behind the Bricklieve mountains: only this afternoon I was climbing there amidst the cairns and 3,000-year-old burial chambers. From the heights, I'd watched Lough Arrow with the wonder of a man who has discovered a new world. Now, in this achingly beautiful light, the sensation is even more powerful.

For an hour past there has been time to sit, to talk (quietly), to watch and, of course, to listen: a badger coughing unaccountably near to us on a darkening isthmus; an owl; a roost of starlings; and now and then the startling slurp of an unseen taking trout. But where, where in all this cauldron of water, will we find our fish and, above all, a hatch of Lough Arrow's famous duck fly?

"We sit," says Rob. "We wait as long as it takes and if we see fish move, we chase them and get close, stalking them all the while." I shiver. "I can see you're cold, but that's not a problem. You see, the duck fly – the black midge to non-anglers – is a creature of cold nights. Their homes are deep down – 40 or even 50 feet down in the pike holes – so perhaps the temperature isn't as important to them as you'd think. The duck fly comes on us quickly here. On April 1st we see the dorsal fins of fish as they sip in the emergers. By the second, they're popping off the dries.

"We wait as long as it takes and if we see fish move, we chase them and get close, stalking them all the while."

ARROW AT SUNSET (opposite) *Although the temperature drops quickly as the sun sets over Lough Arrow, that doesn't stop the duck fly hatching.*

THE STALKER *If you're going to get the very best out of Irish lough fishing, then you've got to put yourself out a bit. It's no good just fishing office hours and hoping for the best, and many's the night when success attends those who stay out until the early hours.*

> *"It's devastating fishing. You can follow a fish, cover it 40 times in 20 minutes and almost hit it on the head – and still nothing."*

"It's devastating fishing. You can follow a fish, cover it 40 times in 20 minutes and almost hit it on the head – and still nothing. Not a shred of interest. Why? Look down. (I do as I'm told.) The answer is right there in front of you. On a square yard of water you'll see a score, no, 50 shucks, perhaps more. There'll be near-spent flies, too, so you can cast 100 times to a fish's nose and there's still no compelling reason he should ever choose yours."

EVENING CONTENTMENT

I ponder on all this, reflecting on a sunset that is now atomic and the meal that I've just wolfed, courtesy of Rob's wife, Stephanie. I'm simply too happy, too much in awe, to fish. There's a brown trout some five yards from me: I can make out its darkly spotted back as he porpoises through the surface film. He's a three-pounder. I shift and eye the rod, but no: there'll be other times for me.

"You ask about the perfect evening for fishing? Flat calm for me. There's a west wind now, not much John, but enough. Watch how I'm having to cast to the east

much more than I'd like to. Fishing that way I lose all the light and I have to fish comparatively blind. But it doesn't matter about the weather because they don't rise each and every night, even though the fly life is always there – always. It is said that the fish have a night on and a night off in succession but I really don't know about that at all. Fishermen's excuses if you ask me – and don't we need those sometimes! I suppose like many things in angling it's all more complex than we're ever likely to understand – the way that temperature changes and oxygen levels combine, for example. But then again, when are we going to chance upon the talking trout?"

I know why I like Rob. He's easy. He takes the fishing and the life in this remote part of the world in his calm, welcoming stride. And, of course, I like his wife, his lodge, his lough, and this incessant, flaming sunset that I thought 10 minutes ago could get no better, but which, now that I've put my camera away, has gone and surpassed itself. But this is no time and no place to be grumpy for no real reason…

"Now! Yes! See the circle of a taking fish? It could be… it could be a perch. No. Of course not. See him there. A brown trout and a good one. He's just finned again and on a calm night we could track every movement, but that's not possible now with this

PASTORAL IDYLL? *The countryside of rural Ireland has not changed dramatically over the centuries, and this can produce problems for the fishing. Unrestricted livestock farming can easily result in the over-enrichment of fragile, aquatic environments.*

wave. Yes, I know he did swirl heavily then, but I swear it's not the boat – it's just that he's engrossed in feeding. I'm not confident. I never am, particularly when fishing the duck fly. I've a spent fly imitation among the real ones and I need more fish up and moving to increase my chances, I guess."

Rob is a sensitive man. Perhaps he picks up that I don't care, that being here is enough. I sense that he does. "We could move on to two or three other places... if I'm out here and the night really calls out to me then I'll fish until midnight or beyond. I love the mobility, the constant attempt to ambush. This is like bone fishing, I guess – predicting the movement of fish all according to the state of the water and the breeze. Getting close to the fish is all about being light on that water, isn't it? Not spooking the fish. Being as one with everything as much as you can manage. The heron didn't become the survivor he is by making mistakes.

LEARNING TO RELAX

"John. You guide, too, don't you? How do you get it across to people that fish can't be bought, that they don't respond to a cheque book? I had an Italian out here with me last year. I'd taken him out like this five times, on better, much better, evenings. We'd seen the water boiling with trout until it seemed they'd consume the boat. Well, wouldn't you know it, he didn't have a sniff, not a single rise to strike at. On his last night we got back to the lodge and he was very quiet. He messed around with his whiskey, fidgeted with a cigar, and then suddenly erupted... 'Rob, I must, I *must* catch me a fish tomorrow.' His arms were waving. His eyes were rolling. It was petrifying!

"All night I wondered about it. Why come to a place like this (Rob opens his arms to a sunset that is now God's own) and put yourself under the pressures of a life that you have left behind? In the morning he came into the kitchen to apologize. He said that it had got to him, that's all. We had a hug and a laugh, and at long last he started to relax. His fishing immediately bucked up as he got into a rhythm and the tension began seeping out of him. And, in the blink of an eye, an angler I had felt was only adequate became good! Naturally, he caught his trout once he realized it didn't matter one way or another."

I wonder how many happy endings Lough Arrow has seen over the years? We dock, Rob loads the electric motor into a rather nifty wheelbarrow and we head back to the nearby lodge. The lights are on, Stephanie has a kettle on the boil and there's a bottle open. "You've got the bedroom overlooking the lough," says Stephanie, and I thank her. "It was always the best and I know this for sure," she laughs. "When we took over four or five years ago, the lodge was in quite a state, totally run down. Nobody had looked after the place for years and the work needed was immense. It could have been disheartening – imagine the wet days and long windy nights wondering if we'd ever make it, ever get the lodge back to what it once was."

> *"How do you get it across to people that fish can't be bought, that they don't respond to a cheque book?"*

THE ADMIRABLE CAPTAIN CRICHTON

"Bringing the Arrow Lodge back to life has been a labour of love and, as you'll see, fascination," continues Stephanie. "When you go upstairs look at your fireplace and you'll notice that the ash-pit is immensely deep. Cleaning it out seemed to be an endless job but, then, virtually when I'd got to the bottom, we came across a number of artefacts, charred but amazingly intact. There was a Farlow's label – you know the famous London tackle manufacturers. Imagine. I rooted about frantically and next came across several letters redirected to the Honourable Captain George Crichton of the Coldstream Guards. There were a couple of invitations, too, one to join Mrs Basil Anstruthers at home at the Hyde Park Hotel where there would be dancing.

"The date and time – 10.30 in the evening on May 30th, 1906 – would have been critical for a fisherman, I suppose. The fact that Captain Crichton had placed the invitation in the fire only indicated that, like any angler now or a century ago, he was happier with the mayfly than with the music. We wonder sometimes what refuge the Edwardian Arrow Lodge offered this man who, we later discovered, had fought and been wounded in the Boer War? When he sat on the lough, he couldn't guess at the trench warfare that would be coming his way in just eight short years."

Upon my return home from Arrow Lodge I hunted out a copy of a Farlow's catalogue of Captain Crichton's time, through the good offices of my friend Chris Samford. The Captain would surely have used Farlow's mayfly patterns, priced between three shillings and sixpence (.24 euro) and six shillings (.43 euro) per dozen. Perhaps he stored them in a trout fly book of hand-sewn pigskin (14 shillings, or 1 euro) or perhaps of Russian leather (13 shillings or .93 euro). Would he have used the Farlow's Mayfly Dapping Rod? Sixteen feet of East Indian cane with a green-heart top (one pound and fifteen shillings or 2.5 euro). Or would he have gone for the Pennel Lake Trout Rod? Light, all green-heart and, at 13 feet, giving him exquisite control for only about 1.5 euro. He may have taken the light split-cane fly rod named after H. T. Sheringham, angling editor of *The Field* (7.15 euro) or perhaps he aspired to a Leonard, the celebrated American's split-bamboo rod at 9.3 euro.

One thing is certain – that a man destined to rise to Colonel, to be decorated with the KCVO, and to become equerry to King George V, would necessarily have shopped with C. Farlow, the eternal Grand Prix winner, the company with shops in St. James's Square and on the Strand.

A MARK OF QUALITY *Farlow, Hardy, Leonard - these are names that are synonymous with quality in angling tackle. We all know that fish can be caught on a bamboo cane, a length of string, and a bent hook, but it's great to fish with the best.*

SNIPPETS OF A LIFE
It's strange to think of an angler sitting in this very room a century ago, thinking of the responsibilities he has put on hold but much more intent upon the weather and the prospects for the day to come.

FISHING LOUGH ARROW

The season on Lough Arrow begins on April 1st and runs to September 30th. If you're fishing during the duck fly season – or in any month, come to that – Arrow is far best attacked by boat. You'll find public access at Brick Pier on the eastern shore, Rinn Ban Pier on the western shore, and Ballinafad Pier to the south. Private access points should only be used with the owner's permission. Most of Arrow is quite deep, so safety isn't a big issue in many areas. However, be careful in bays and especially when approaching the points of headlands and islands. Be warned… there are large shallow rocky areas around Dodd's Shore and Hargadon's Point, and south of Andresna Point. Keep your eyes open also for the distinctive rock markers, not that every potential danger is marked like this. As ever, it's always wise to go out with a local guide for the first few visits.

Boatmanship is very important indeed, almost as crucial as fishing skills themselves. Not only do you have to locate the best places on the lough, but it's also important not to scare the fish. You've also got to manoeuvre the boat into the best possible fishing position… none of this is easy, especially in a stiff breeze. On calm, cool nights in April when fishing the duck fly rise, Rob uses his electric motor and this gives a definite advantage over oars because it's quiet and it allows him to fish and to stalk rising trout at the same time. It's possible that foot controls, the norm in American-style boats, would make manoeuvrability even easier.

The duck fly, a species of chironomid, is the first major fly to hatch on Lough Arrow. It begins to appear in mid-April and lasts for about three weeks. It's most prolific in the evenings, from around 7 o'clock, but sometimes in favourable weather conditions you will see them hatching during the day. Fishing during the duck fly period is all about the weather. In windy weather, when there's a good chop on the water, most anglers prefer wet fly tactics. Use flies such as the Sooty Olive, the Claret Bumble, the Connemara Black, the Peter Ross, and Silver Invicta. Hook sizes 10, 12, and even 14 are preferred.

It's on those still evenings that the real excitement begins when, like Rob, you can stalk individual fish using small buzzers and emergers on long, light leaders. Twelve feet is about ideal, with a breaking strain of four pounds at the point… not less, because some Arrow trout can reach six pounds or more. A nine-foot rod with a five-weight floating line completes the outfit. The last hour of daylight is particularly effective, and do be prepared to stay late if necessary. It can get cold at this time of the year, so make sure you're well rugged up and even take a flask of coffee. If the cold forces

FISHING THE SURFACE FILM *Suspenders, emergers, buzzers; there's a whole reawakening of interest in pursuing trout in that magical dimension of the surface film. It's here that so many insects are trapped and, as they struggle to free themselves, offer an easy meal.*

you in, you could be missing the best of the action. A hat is also useful against the midges, and don't forget a good torch if you're planning to stay out late. Always wear either Polaroids or transparent safety glasses when fly fishing, especially when using a long leader and there's any breeze about, because accidents can happen.

Of course, Arrow isn't just about the duck fly and it fishes superbly throughout the season. The olives start to appear in the first two weeks of May, and around the 20th of the month the mayfly begin to hatch. At the same time as the mayfly hatch, the evening buzzer fishing really takes off as well. There's some excellent sedge fishing, especially during the last two weeks of July when the Green Peters emerge. At first, the Peters appear late in the day, certainly after 10 o'clock, but by the end of July or early August, you can be fishing as early as half past eight.

Arrow also has a limited hatch of murrough or the great red sedge. You'll find these huge flies hatching in bays, close to islands and around rocky outcrops. There's a lot of surface activity once the hatch begins after dusk… try to fish westwards to make the most use of the prevailing light. Also, be prepared to stay late – you shouldn't think of coming in before midnight if you're a serious lough fisherman.

SURFACE RAIDER *Big fish, especially, will look for calm areas of water where the surface film is at its thickest. It's here that flies have the greatest problem in breaking free of the water and bursting into the air. Trout can take their time examining insects before making a decision about their acceptability.*

GREAT RED SEDGE

LOUGH INAGH
The Old and the New

Lough Inagh Lodge is the stones and mortar of Irish piscatorial history. It's set in a landscape that, apart from some forestry, has remained largely unchanged for centuries. It is perhaps apt that the lodge is the heart of a community called Recess – certainly it's a place to chat with ghosts. The lodge today is elegant but uncluttered, firmly in tune with its history. The bar is a good place to sit, maybe in front of the fire, and ponder the past. The many black and white photographs depict an age before the advent of the internal combustion engine and black-top roads. They seem to come from a period long ago, but the history we're talking about isn't as old as you'd think: many of Ireland's oldest ghillies remember times without electricity with ease. Their fathers witnessed the coming of the motorcar as young men, and their grandfathers could have been born during the potato famine, when Peel was Prime Minister and Queen Victoria had been on the throne for less than 10 years.

Ireland's fishing in the early years of the 21st century is rightly considered to be special by anglers worldwide, but the fishing here has always been special. After the potato famine of the 1840s, the population of Ireland dropped from nine million to three million, the countryside was quieter than ever, and any pressure that there may have been on the fisheries virtually disappeared. The threat of rotten potatoes continued for a long time after 1847, however, breathing into the Irish people a

"The many black and white photographs... seem to come from a period long ago, but the history we're talking about isn't as old as you'd think."

BROODING PERFECTION (opposite) *Not a breath of wind stirs the surface of the lough. Fishing a mirror like this is notoriously hard: try a large dry fly, twitched occasionally to impart life; or fish a team of imitative flies down deep on a very long leader.*

FROZEN IN TIME *The far west of Ireland has always been a fly fisher's Mecca. Anglers from the past returning to Inagh Lodge, even after a century, would notice little difference – apart perhaps from the fishing, which is arguably even better!*

THE PERFECT SETTING *The fishing lodge is a magnificent creation. It affords a total escape from the real world, where an angler can immerse him- or herself in what is truly important in life. It's a place to recharge the batteries, or even one in which to discover your true identity.*

toughness that those who know them well are quick to recognize and admire. Until recently, Ireland might well have been a poor country, but the Irish themselves have always shown the dignity of self-employed people. Traditionally, they've worked very hard for little money, but show any Irishman the light at the end of the tunnel and he will make the very most use of it. It's no coincidence that the Irish have proved to be the most successful ethnic group in the United States: they may have arrived as paupers, but they became founding fathers of some of the richest American families.

Tradition and Knowledge

Fishing in Ireland is only in part about the fish themselves and the remarkable scenery. Everyone who goes there appreciates the Irish, and Irish fellow fishermen above all. You will find that they share what they have, and a day on Inagh will often prove this. Spot a campfire coming from one of the islands and stop for a chat: chances are you'll be made a partner in whatever food and drink are available.

Those who know the Inagh fishery intimately today, like Colin Folan, the resident guide here, realize that many things never change. Be it the end of the 19th century or the beginning of the 21st, these waters fish best after a big rain, not from the west or the east, because that doesn't catch in the valley, but from the north or the south so that it settles and has maximum impact. Colin knows, too, that Lough Inagh needs a northerly or southerly to fish its best: go out in any other and the wind will be everywhere and, if high, spinning the boat through 360 degrees, drenching you in water spouts and spelling danger. So much traditional knowledge – how could you pitch up at Inagh as a newcomer and not have a guide? "You need a wind on the river to move your flies; on the lough you'll find the sea trout in the middle, not on the shores like the salmon that follow the points of the islands – investigate the reed beds and the bays; you'll find the sea trout come in on or around St John's Eve (June 23rd) when a new moon, a spring tide, and a bit of rain will see the river sparkle with fish; look at the cormorant rock, just there – see the white of their droppings? That needs to be covered by water if you're to stand a chance. There's no point going out until there's at least an 18-inch rise."

AS IT EVER WAS *Always elegant, almost cathedral-like, Inagh Lodge has hosted battalions of anglers over the centuries and still offers its hospitality to new generations.*

WELCOMING THE NEW

So much knowledge is handed down from father to son, but Colin is never blinkered by the traditional or blind to new developments. Here is a man pioneering modern skills in buzzer fishing for the Irish lough scene. He is mesmerized, as the brownies are, by the epoxy imitations – so slim, so delicate, slicked with coats of varnish that give a shifting, indescribable sheen. The excitement of sight fishing, of watching the action in the surface film, grips him. It's all so close, so intimate, so intense.

Something similar is happening with the River Inagh sea trout – a new, more gentle approach. "I don't say this to you to brag, but because it is true, to make a point. When the sea trout come into the river, they'll stay in the Trout Pool, for instance, two or three days. Now you show me the best night angler and I'll guarantee I can double his catch by fishing in the day with a little orange and amber Klinkhammer.

"Don't look surprised. It's not my skill particularly, but rather the way those sea trout behave. Think how quiet the Trout Pool is, sheltered by forestry, running gentle and calm. Consider how alert sea trout are at night, how alive they become then, how aware they are of anything and everything. They can pick out the most sparsely tied size 14 black Pennell on the darkest of nights, if you need proof of that! So, your man goes out in the last of the light. He's using typical sea trout gear, along with leaders of

"If the angling is changing around Inagh, so are the waters. Nature is too complex not to be constantly in flux."

32 Lough Inagh

eight or ten pounds and a team of wets. He works down the pool, with the splashing of the fly line, the commotion of the flies. He works all the water methodically, there's not a patch undisturbed. And the fish are freaked out of their heads.

"Now, I come along in the daylight. I've got the lightest of gear and just a little fly. I take my time and move as lightly as possible, prepared to wait for fish and stalking them as ghost-like as I can when a fish shows. So, I see a sea trout move and I slide into position to cover him at once, upstream so he doesn't see me or pick up on the line. He's mine. So is the next – and the next. Beautiful, bright fish, and one goes two and a half pounds. Of course, they all go back, just that bit wiser for the experience."

THREATS AND CHALLENGES

If the angling is changing around Inagh, so, too, are the waters. Nature is too complex not to be constantly in flux. The aquatic environment faces a host of problems, but it survives and adapts because of the endless possibilities: at Inagh, in common with many Irish fisheries, the dangers are posed by our own clumsy actions.

"As kids we never bothered with the browns in the lough. The water was acidic and the fish only had terrestrials such as hoppers or moths to live on. If my dad or I got a 12-ounce fish, we were surprised. Now there are five pounders and bigger fish, buckets of them. They even average one to two pounds now. So what's happened? Well, because of the fish farms, the estuaries are infested with sea lice – clouds and clouds of them. Now, sea trout are only brown trout going to the sea to earn a living, after all, so what do the smolts do when faced with the lice and probable death? Some fight on, but a good many turn back to freshwater and the lough.

"Here, too, we've tinkered with things. The pH level of the water has changed because of forestation. Now, because the lough is a richer place, with fabulous amounts of mayfly, sedge, and olives, those trout denied the sea can still thrive, but without the travelling. And there's a last factor to look at… this time a natural one. Although the lough is shallow, there are big shoals of char present. Yes, I can see by the look on your face that you've got it. Those thwarted sea trout can grow to two pounds or so on the fly life and then become predatory on the char that average just a few ounces. Suddenly, out of nothing, Lough Inagh has stocks of 'newly-hatched' ferox trout! What this means for the fisherman is that you can walk the shores, watching for a rise, cover it, and catch the finest wild, brown trout in the world. Don't get me wrong. I detest fish farms, netting, anything that harms the fish runs that we've been blessed with, but God does work in the most mysterious of ways."

In many respects, despite the rock solidity of Inagh Lodge and all it stands for, Colin is part of a changing world. Certainly the Irish ghillie is a figure making his way into the sunset. "I'm here from May until the end of the season: I'm the resident guide. My father will come in to help, along with a really skilled team of internationals and fly creators. They are my assistant guides. We are only like the ghillies from the

PARADISE FOUND *The hill, the stream, the bridge, the pool; it's a fishing rod that transports you to such wonderful places where it's quite enough to sit, watch, and brood upon the majesty of nature. Of course, it's always nice to catch a fish too!*

BRIGHT WATERS (opposite) *Brown trout are supremely adaptable, but ideally they love clean water, sparkling gravel, vibrant weed, and oxygen-rich currents. Wild fish like this are the source of Ireland's fly-fishing fame.*

past in that we have a deep knowledge of the waters. We've moved on from those men, because we have real skills that we can impart to the visitors. We care for the fish hugely and this comes across, too. Of course, we'll give them the best of the fishing, but we'll satisfy deeper objectives as well. We'll perhaps help them with casting problems, or explaining the life cycle of the mayfly. We'll help them read waters completely anew. We'll give them more chance to enjoy the day in a full and meaningful way. If it's blazing hot, for instance, and not a fish is moving in fresh water, we can take the guests down to the estuary and get them fishing for mackerel on the fly. A big streamer, a floating line, and a sink tip, and you'll have the time of your life. A slow retrieve and... fireworks. Forget a team of flies: hook three mackerel at once and you can kiss that rod goodbye!

"There are other changes, too, at the heart of Irish fishing. We insist on catch-and-release for our sea trout and browns, and the numbers and size have both increased. Now the fish are allowed to spawn, to get out, and hopefully to come back again. In the last year we've had lots of two-and-a-half-pound fish, and we're hoping for far more to come. With the foreign and British anglers we've had, there's been no problem insisting on catch-and-release for some time, and now it's the same with the Irish themselves. The Irish fly-fishing scene is now serious. We use the best tackle and have the best waders. We've caught up, at the very least, and the old images of the shabby wormer with a bagful of corpses is a thing of the past. Dubliners, especially, just used to fish Lough Corrib for the plate, but now more and more fish go back. And there's huge sympathy for the plight of the sea trout and what they face at the hands of the fish farmers. Of course, I'd still like to see size limits go up and the sale of wild fish completely banned. We don't want to end up like the English, destroying most of our wild fisheries and then trying to reinstate them when, for many, it's just too late. We've got a jewel here that we all want to look after."

"Forget a team of flies: hook three mackerel at once and you can kiss that rod goodbye!"

THE STICK AND THE STONE *Yet again, not a hint of a breeze disturbs the surface of the lough. Sometimes it's best to admit defeat, head for the nearby coastline, and flick out a gaudy fly or two in the hope of a passing mackerel shoal.*

Colin's Inagh Advice

Colin sits on the wall at the Derryclare Butts and looks down where the inner river enters the lake. This is perhaps his favourite place, his "banker" for duffers like me. He reels off some of the tips for this magical fishery…

- For sea trout, you need around a 10-foot, 7- to 8-weight rod. A weight forward 7 line is fine, with a 6- to 8-lb cast.

- The same will pass for the salmon that average just under 10 pounds but can approach the teens.

- For salmon in the river, an 8-lb leader will do, but replace this with a 10- or 12-lb leader if the river is running high.

- For salmon on the lough, try a three fly team: a Daddy or Claret Bumble on the top, a Green Dabbler or Green Peter in the middle, and a Thunder and Lightning or Black Pennell at the tail. Tie them all on a size 10.

- Throw them around 15 yards and fish traditional lough, wet-fly style. Don't forget to bob the top fly close to the boat and don't strike but tighten up on a take.

- In the river, try a Silver Badger, a Silver Rat, or a Silver Stoat – singles or doubles, sizes 10 or 12.

- Later in the season an Ally's Shrimp on a size 12 is worth a try.

COLIN'S COLLIE DOG TIP

A 1¼-inch Collie, preferably a Red Throat, is the best fly for any time of the year, in any water conditions, at any water level! You'll fish it on a 12-foot rod with a 5-foot braid leader attached to a 12-foot tippet of 12-lb nylon. But listen. You first fish the pool conventionally with size 10s. Nothing? Go lighter and fish it with size 12s. Still blanking?

Try the third attack with simple trout flies. Nothing? Well, finally, take out the Collie Dog outfit. You've built up to the last ditch approach. Try a cast across and slightly upstream. Strip back as fast as you can. Really whip that Collie back, and any fish that have shown limited interest in your flies daylong will go frantic for it. Or not. If the Collie doesn't work, you might just as well go home!

BALLYNAHINCH
Castle, River, and Lough

"Such magic – the evenings outside the castle after dinner in the half-light, the first bats whirling around..."

Let's do this the way the sea trout and the salmon would, looking first at the sea, then at the estuary mouth at Roundstone, just to the south of Ballynahinch Castle. It's here that you begin to sense the magic and see the beauty. On a bright, crisp spring day, Roundstone shimmers in the light. Just out of season, some of the bars and shops are closed, but there's still plenty of life: the tide is out and fishermen are working on their nets, boats, and pots. There's a tang of salt in the air. Gulls call constantly, numerous as snowflakes against the blue. The freshness of the place rides on the wind: nothing here is cramped, dark, or restricted, and it's easy to imagine the wild silver fish heading homewards with the incoming tide.

At first the road to Ballynahinch rises only a little as it crosses the desolate, flat plain studded with small pools and streams, but soon the grandeur of the Twelve Pins mountain range looms into sight. You are following the river now, the Ballynahinch itself, with a maze of casting piers covering all the pools. And then you're into a magical island, one of indigenous oak and beech woodland and a hundred shades of green. Finally, Ballynahinch Castle itself, for decades the angler's dream, the home of the luckiest sea trout fishers in the world, comes into view.

A Past Age of Romance

"You'd hardly believe now how it once was here. Sixty years ago, which I can remember, right up until 15 years ago or thereabouts, which I'd sometimes rather forget. Such magic – the evenings outside the castle after dinner in the half-light, the first bats whirling around, the sound of a piano from a drawing room, laughter coming from the open windows, for the best sea trout weather was always warm. Then I would take my fishermen down to the river, down in amongst the gardens, and the water would be alive with fish. Salmon – and sea trout, of course – in endless numbers. Great, golden ripples spreading across the sunset. Glorious it was, I tell you – the perfume of the flowers, the singing of the river. And we would catch fish, everyone would, beginner or expert. It was an angler's Paradise, that river, that setting, those fish. Believe me, it was Heaven on Earth. Long nights afterwards with the fish on the slab in the bar, over there by the scales. You couldn't believe it would ever come to an end." So speaks Mike Conneely, the former head fishing guide at Ballynahinch Castle, with deep regret at the passing of an era.

Much of Ballynahinch's history reads like the wildest of romances, especially the 1920s and 1930s, when so much of Ballynahinch's present character was formed. In 1924, Ballynahinch was bought by His Highness the Maharaja Jam Sahib of

GLORIOUS IT WAS *In the Ballynahinch bar, where he's known such happy times his life through, Mike recalls his days as head fishing guide with pleasure.*

DESIGNER RIVER (opposite) *The river here is a delightful combination of wilderness and sensitive management. The pools are historic, and the fishermen who've enjoyed them are legendary. Ballynahinch is liquid history.*

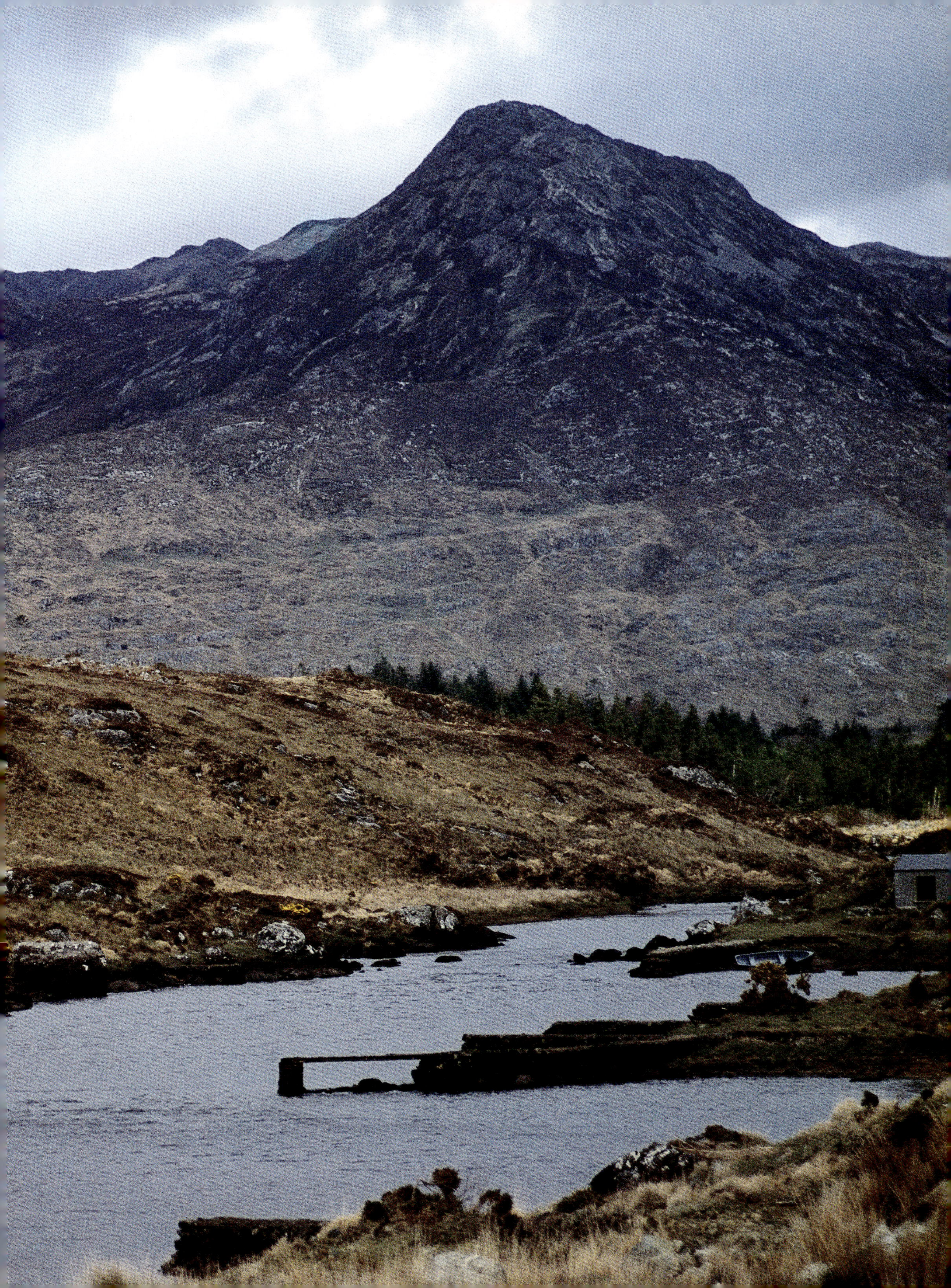

Ballynahinch

> "Ranji's bank balance electrified Ballynahinch: his arrival at the castle... was the event for which many of the locals lived."

RANJI IN HIS FINERY *Fishing is important in all countries that aren't solely desert. It is a central link between the past and the present that remains as strong as ever, but there is no doubt that fishing is more deeply rooted in the past in Ireland than in any other country of the world.*

Nawangar or, as he became known more simply, Ranji. A test cricketer, hunter, soldier, statesman, and quite fanatical fisherman, Ranji was to have a huge impact on both the scenery and the psyche of this part of Connemara. It was during his decade at Ballynahinch that the gardens and woods were landscaped, and that the piers and fishing huts we see today were established. It's hard to grasp the wealth of the Indian royalty: it was recently put to me that, even today, if all the gold owned by the royal families of India were melted down, the glut would make the metal worthless throughout the world. Certainly, Ranji's bank balance electrified Ballynahinch: his arrival at the castle in June for the forthcoming season was the event for which many of the locals lived. He travelled from Galway by train, and firecrackers were placed on the track to herald his arrival at the station just half a mile from the castle itself. On board would be his Indian retinue, as well as a fleet of cars bought new in Galway each season and given away at the end to such local dignitaries as the vicar, the priest, or the doctor. The avenue up to the castle was covered with marble chips that were raked each day so that the route glittered in the sunshine. Every year, on Ranji's birthday, a party was held for all his staff. In the billiard room, which is now the hotel bar, the Maharaja himself served the food, the beer, and the wine until the intoxicated could only just make it to the truck commandeered to drive them home. Staunchly loyal to George V, Ranji always wished to toast the sovereign on such occasions, but he knew that such a thing would cause havoc in those wildly republican days. Instead, the throng would be asked to raise their glasses to the Emperor of India and enthusiastic toasts were drunk, unsuspectingly, to the grandson of Queen Victoria, the first Empress of India!

For the rest of the time, Ranji was not a social animal but was dedicated to his fishing, which he pursued from dawn to dusk, day in, day out. It's not unusual for cricketers to enjoy field sports, and when Ranji lost the sight of his right eye in a shooting accident he turned quite naturally to fly fishing. Nawangar is in Uttar Pradesh, close to the tributaries of the Ganges that flow from the Himalayas. Many trout had been stocked in this region, brought over from Britain as eggs and fingerlings in Ranji's boyhood, and by the time he was a young man, the brown trout fishing in Kashmir had become legendary, so it's no surprise to find that a man with his wealth and passion should want to seek out the best fly fishing in the world. Ballynahinch offered just that.

If you can, go and visit Ranji's Rock, a well-known point on beat seven. It's a wild, lonely, and lovely spot, and it's easy to see why it was the Indian's favourite stretch of the river. Perhaps, as they say, he does still haunt the place, living again and again his successes, perhaps wishing to undo one failure. Frank Cummings was his long-time guide on the water, and he was there on that particular evening... "Sir, sir, please, you must give him line. Sir, let him go, you must sir. Sir, sir... you stupid, deaf bugger you... will you bloody well listen to what I tell you in the future?"

And then, at the start of the 1990s, this earthly Paradise of the Ranji, of Mike Conneely, Frank Cummings, and untold thousands of anglers like them, fell apart. Would Ballynahinch ever again be the Mecca for sea-trout fishers worldwide?

ROOMS WITH A VIEW *The castle, the grounds, and the river would grace any film set. Their beauty has a dreamlike quality and, once having fished there, it's impossible ever to forget the experience.*

MODERN MANAGEMENT AT BALLYNAHINCH

Alan Sullivan is the fishery manager at Ballynahinch today. He's highly trained, well travelled and has a well-developed philosophy for the renewal of the fishery. "You've got to understand the bottom fell out of Mike's world in 1990. 1989 was the last good year – the records indicate 4,000 sea trout and 445 salmon being caught. Then, the following season, just 23 fish came from the hotel water. Of course, this is all about the impact of the fish farms and the appalling conditions they create in the estuaries. We've had a decade of frustrations, pitching ourselves constantly against the scientific frailties of their arguments, but there's light at the end of the tunnel. The fishing may never be quite as fantastic again, but it's good now and getting better. There's a real chance to do something positive. I'm trying to do three things – care for the fishery, for the guests, and for the locals. I like to think it's a solid concept, a real overview where everything dovetails to make sense – an environmental jigsaw puzzle, if you like.

"What everybody's got to realize is that Ballynahinch is simply special. Period. No argument. Of course, it's a heavily managed environment and represents an oasis of care. If you look at the grounds around the castle, you'll appreciate the indigenous Irish woodland that grows in abundance. You can tell immediately where Ballynahinch's demarcation line lies because the landscape instantly becomes grazed to smithereens by sheep. This is not how Ireland used to be historically, when it was treed as Ballynahinch is today, and this alone makes what we've got unique and special. We might never see the bar slab piled high with fish again, as it was in the 1980s, but that shouldn't matter. It's not just the fishing here – it's the place.

"Everything we're trying to do is more modern, more streamlined. For example, we'll begin the fishing at the start of the week with an interview, asking what the guests' objectives are. We've totally moved away from the antiquated ghillie ideology. The men we have working here are guides, taking people out for the day, imparting their vast knowledge to them. If the fishing isn't great, then they will tweak casting skills, explain the character of the river, or the life-cycle of the fish or the flies. There is a new sense of professionalism, of an opportunity to pass on knowledge.

"And the anglers are responding. The number of people coming in is unbelievable: a lot of first time anglers, including women. Anglers aren't just coming here now to empty the river, but to enjoy an historical environment and to learn deeply about it. People don't want to kill fish now, as they once did, and we encourage handling skills. From mid-June onwards, you will catch sea trout at Ballynahinch most evenings: they will average only a pound or so, but you will get them to two and a half pounds or more. We don't allow fishing at night, because we need the daylight to watch how fish are handled and to make sure they are returned safely.

COMRADES IN ARMS *Happy days, happy lives, happy memories. It doesn't matter where you fish in Ireland, you can guarantee that the waters will boast a dynasty of ghillies and a tapestry of knowledge passed on for a century or more from great grandfathers to sons.*

"You'll see salmon, too, and last year 300 were hooked. This is the downside, the one time you rather miss the period of the "professional" fishermen – only 79 of them were landed, largely because so many of the anglers were beginners who simply could not cope with such large, powerful fish. It's then that you have to be diplomatic and explain gently that expertise isn't something that just comes with a credit card.

"Ballynahinch and its fishery don't exist in a vacuum. To succeed, it's got to become very much a part of the local community. I see a three-tier price structure for tourists, Irish nationals, and locals. You can't fight the locals – that would be an impossible battle and, anyway, they hold the key to anything that can be achieved. For example, we're committed here to building buffer zones around the nursery areas. This means tree planting and stock control, so it's imperative to win over the farmers. We have to show the people themselves that real good that can come from schemes like this. There'll be more fish, more fishermen, and more real jobs as a result. This is our handle, the way we've got to sell schemes that might initially appear unpopular.

"I like to get the local kids in and walk the forest and the river, explaining what's special about them. I show them the rubbish that the adults – sometimes their own parents – have left, and when they see it scarring such a special environment it hits home. They see what you're getting at. It's tremendously satisfying. I see the long-term future of Ballynahinch with great optimism. With tender loving care, the fishing will continue to get better and better, and modern-thinking anglers will flock here, creating long-term, sustained employment. By caring for, and enhancing, the environment, everyone is going to win out."

LOW WATER *Of course, even in Paradise, conditions have to be right, and low water is a hard problem to overcome. Try fishing early and late. Fish slightly lighter. Cast even more delicately than usual. Concentrate harder than ever, so that if you do get a chance then you make it count.*

RIVER SEA-TROUT FISHING

The cream of sea-trout fishing is very frequently on falling water at anytime from late April through to September. Early on in the season, floating or intermediate lines can be used with larger flies – something like a small Silver Doctor is fine. As summer moves on, falling water continues to be the prime time, but the flies become smaller – Black Pennells are hard to beat in sizes 8 or 10.

Sea trout can also be caught during the day in the long, still pools that you'll find them frequenting. They have to be stalked and your movements must be heron-like. A floating line and small dry flies work well if you see any fish moving. If the sea trout are deeper, then small Connemara Blacks and Black Pennells work well tied on a size 12 or 14. Let the flies sink slowly with the current. If the pool is really still, move them back slowly with a very gentle figure-of-eight technique. Your every movement has to be carefully and thoughtfully executed. Use every shred of bankside cover that you can.

Sea trout generally become more active as the light begins to fade and dusk pulls in. This is a particularly killing period at Ballynahinch. The best nights are calm and still, often muggy and sultry. Sadly, they also prove to be the prime time for midges, so you'll probably need a net and certainly lotion. Remember to put it on the backs of your hands and wrists.

If true night fishing is allowed, it always pays to do a very thorough recce of the stretch of river that you're going to be fishing. If the night is dark – and moonless nights are the best – you need to know where any potential hazards along the bank are situated. You also need to be quite sure about the structure of the pools and where there are potentially dangerous snags. Take your time. Wait until it's really dark. Don't approach a pool too early, or you could spook it for the rest of the night. Bear in mind that a number of fish may have moved into the neck of the pool where the water is skinny, or may even be moving around the shallow margins. If they see you, they'll be off spreading the news.

It's not a difficult technique – coping with the darkness is the true challenge. A floating line is the norm, with flies such as the Butcher, Silver Doctor, or Black Pennell. Simply cast across the stream and mend the line as the flies swing round. Retrieve them slowly through the slack water and repeat the process, slowly covering the pool. Remember that the eyesight of the sea trout is astonishing, even on a dark night, so move with caution, just as you would in the day.

Hugh Falkus is still regarded as the giant of night sea trout tactics, and he saw the sport divided into three main taking periods. He defined the first half as from dusk to around midnight, the second half from 1.30am until daybreak, and the hour of sunrise as extra time! His experience suggested that the height of activity was in the first period, when takes can be vicious but are frequently missed. Sport dies around midnight and it's easy to think that the night is finished. Instead, use the next hour or so to recuperate. Have a snack. Have some coffee. Enjoy the evening. The second half of the night sees the fish less active, down deeper, and frequently best targeted with a sinking line. Sunrise can see a last spurt of activity and, don't forget, it's also probably the best time of the day to hook into a salmon. That is, if you've got the energy to land it!

CARAGH AND CLOON
Glencar House Hotel

Lodges anywhere – in Ireland, America, New Zealand, or Argentina – can be so lordly that a tie, even a bow tie, can be as important as a rod and a reel. Of course, there is nothing wrong in this: a certain style is to be applauded, and it in no way detracts from the quality of the fishing or the skill of the anglers. You don't have to walk the halls in an old jacket and patched slippers to be a master fisher, but there are those fishing houses that are relaxed about standards, that accept that time taken in dressing is time off the riverbank, that effort expended in tying a tie could just as well be spent creating a Black Pennell. This is largely the way of things at Glencar House: it is a beautiful building, exquisitely maintained in a sumptuous setting, but it's a working fishing lodge. The anglers I have met there have made the long journey to fish, not to preen, and although they're not shabby, there is that feel of the "lived-in" about their general attire. And, importantly, there's a gong!

I like hotels with gongs. Gongs, hungry anglers, and satisfying repasts have gone hand in hand throughout the happiest days of my life. Towards gong time you sense anticipation: the anglers, mostly men, certainly early in the season here, are in the bar, flicking looks at their watches, shuffling just that little bit closer to the door should they happen to see a member of the dining staff pass. They're listening to each other, for sure, but also to the rumblings in their stomachs and, of course, for the first

"Gongs, hungry anglers, and satisfying repasts have gone hand in hand throughout the happiest days of my life."

IN THE WILDS (opposite) *Glencar truly stands for an Ireland that has all but disappeared. This is a place to get back to the roots of the country and to remember exactly what isolation once meant.*

TIME LOST *The fishing in Ireland remains excellent right into the 21st century, but it's essential when you visit that you take something else on board: the soul-enhancing beauty of a place that has inspired poets, painters, and piscators for a very long time.*

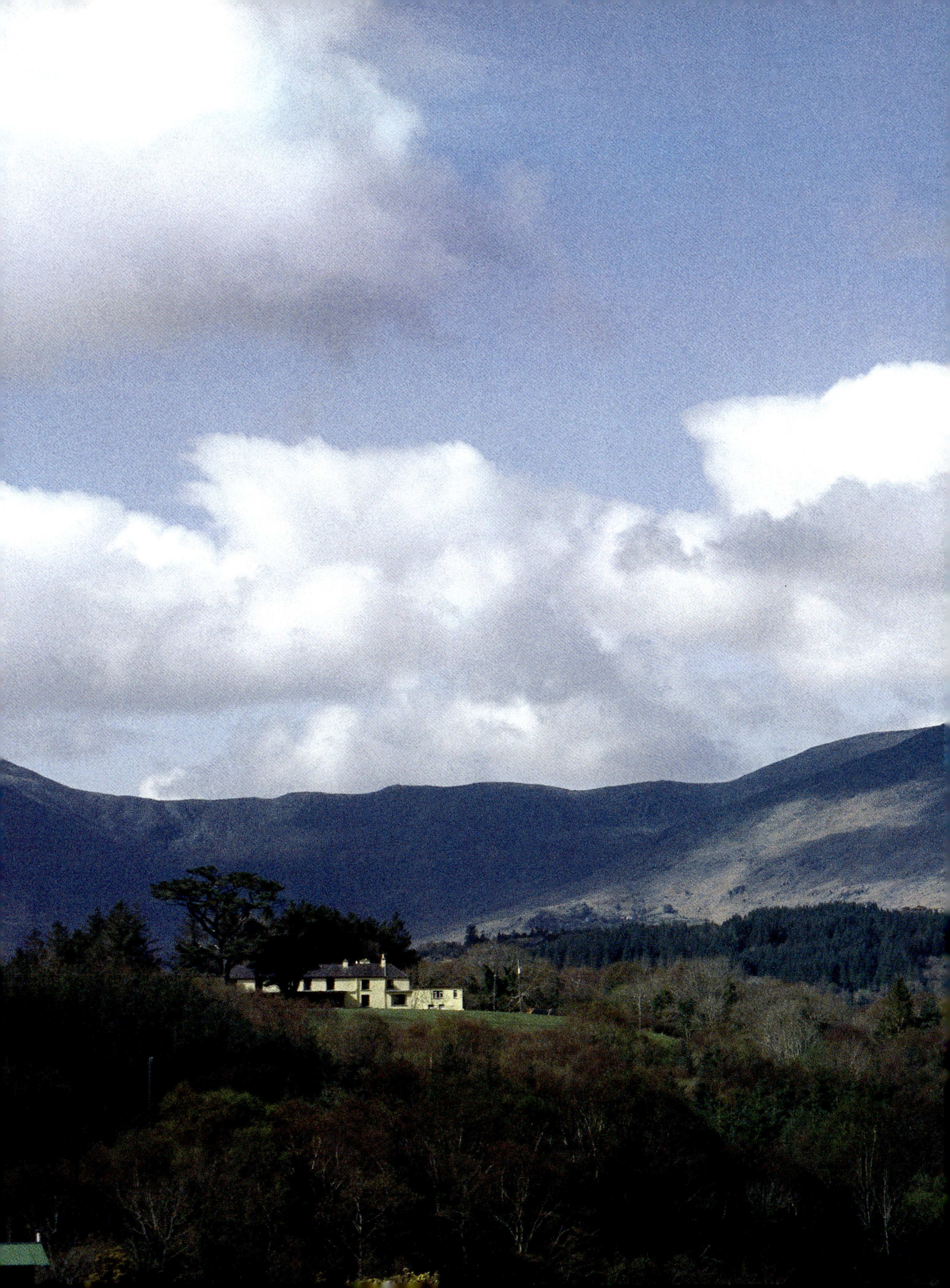

sound of the gong. Ah! The sonorous tones ring down the passageway and the anglers are off. It's not unseemly haste, of course, but the steely determination to be in there first is pointed. Look carefully at the gong and you will realize that it has been there for decades: it has boomed out dinner, season after season, to the faithful who keep returning. And, of course, that these anglers do return as regularly as the salmon themselves speaks volumes about Glencar and the fishing it has to offer.

SET IN A TIMELESS LANDSCAPE

A thorough knowledge of Glencar, its river, and the life around pays huge dividends – but don't go thinking that this is a place that opens up easily or instantly. It is as lost and as secretive a piece of Ireland as you'll find in the 21st century. We really are in the fastnesses of Kerry now. Of course, the modern world is here, or hereabouts, but it's not long ago that the first phones rang, that the electricity was first switched on, that carts and bicycles still out-numbered cars. The fishery office and store shed at Glencar was for years used as a local cinema, for how else would the young men and women find anywhere to do their courting once the autumn winds blew with the harshness of coming winter? The times are not long gone when every cottage would grow its own potatoes and vegetables, when each family owned a single pig – "the man who pays the rent" – to be slaughtered in honour of the bailiff's annual visit. Today sheep still munch the grass around most of the front doors, and even a cursory glance suggests that there's still a cow to every acre.

Glencar is venerability itself, sticking to traditions of welcome, comfort, and solid fishing. It has owned its waters since 1916 – the upper River Caragh where it enters the Lough, and upstream as far as Cloon and Reagh Loughs. Ownership hasn't always been easy: hereabouts in Kerry, republicanism has long flourished and the imposition of alien sporting rights has, I guess, at times sat uneasily on a population wedded to the land and to fierce independence.

Vincent, the manager of the fishery, born and bred in the district, has learnt to walk the tightrope. If, at certain times, a pool is not being fished by guests, and a local farmer with rod and line, or a teenager whose parents want to keep him out of bother, or an old local angler with an afternoon to spare and a yen for a trout supper should wish for an hour or two... well, why not? It's the men with the nets, the four-wheel drives, and a ready market for fresh salmon in the towns and hotels that Vincent and his heir apparent, Michael, are at war with. Over the years, this salmon system has edged from the vibrant to the vulnerable, and there has to be fair play. And it is for this reason that Lough Reagh, at the head of the system and the ultimate destination for many of the salmon, is not fished at all. Vincent smiles. If the salmon get that far, he feels, then they deserve to be left in peace.

Even if you are not allowed a rod there, the walk across the fields to Lough Reagh is worth the effort. Drive to Glencar's boathouse on Cloon, fish a while, and then take

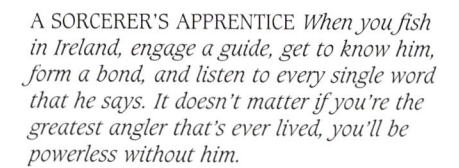

"Glencar is venerability itself, sticking to traditions of welcome, comfort, and solid fishing."

A SORCERER'S APPRENTICE *When you fish in Ireland, engage a guide, get to know him, form a bond, and listen to every single word that he says. It doesn't matter if you're the greatest angler that's ever lived, you'll be powerless without him.*

yourself along the track to the head of the valley. Do this even if the trout or salmon are biting, and even though Cloon itself is one of the most lost and lovely loughs you are ever likely to stumble upon. Soon you will see a clutch of farms, and the inevitable barking dog bounds to greet you and offers its tummy when you smile. Follow the dwindling Caragh, just a stream now, past the ancient graves and there, framed by an amphitheatre of mountains, you'll find Reagh. If you have a soul, you will understand why fish want so badly to run here: this is simply a place as wild as God made it.

Today, a handful of farmers tend their animals but, judging from the number of abandoned cottages, this valley was once much more heavily populated. And, considering the evidence of the many ancient graves, such was the case for centuries, even millennia. No doubt the shelter afforded by those guardian mountains must have been a consideration, along with the alluring mix of high and low pasture. Equally surely, the infant Caragh river with its bestowal of salmon, year after year, from late summer through to the coming of winter, must have been central to life here. Imagine that huge boost of God-given protein as the year waned and the struggle for survival

ALWAYS A CHANCE *Even in low water you can still pick fish up if you target exactly the sorts of places they're likely to be living in. Look for any water that's on the move: the tail of a pool like this is perfect.*

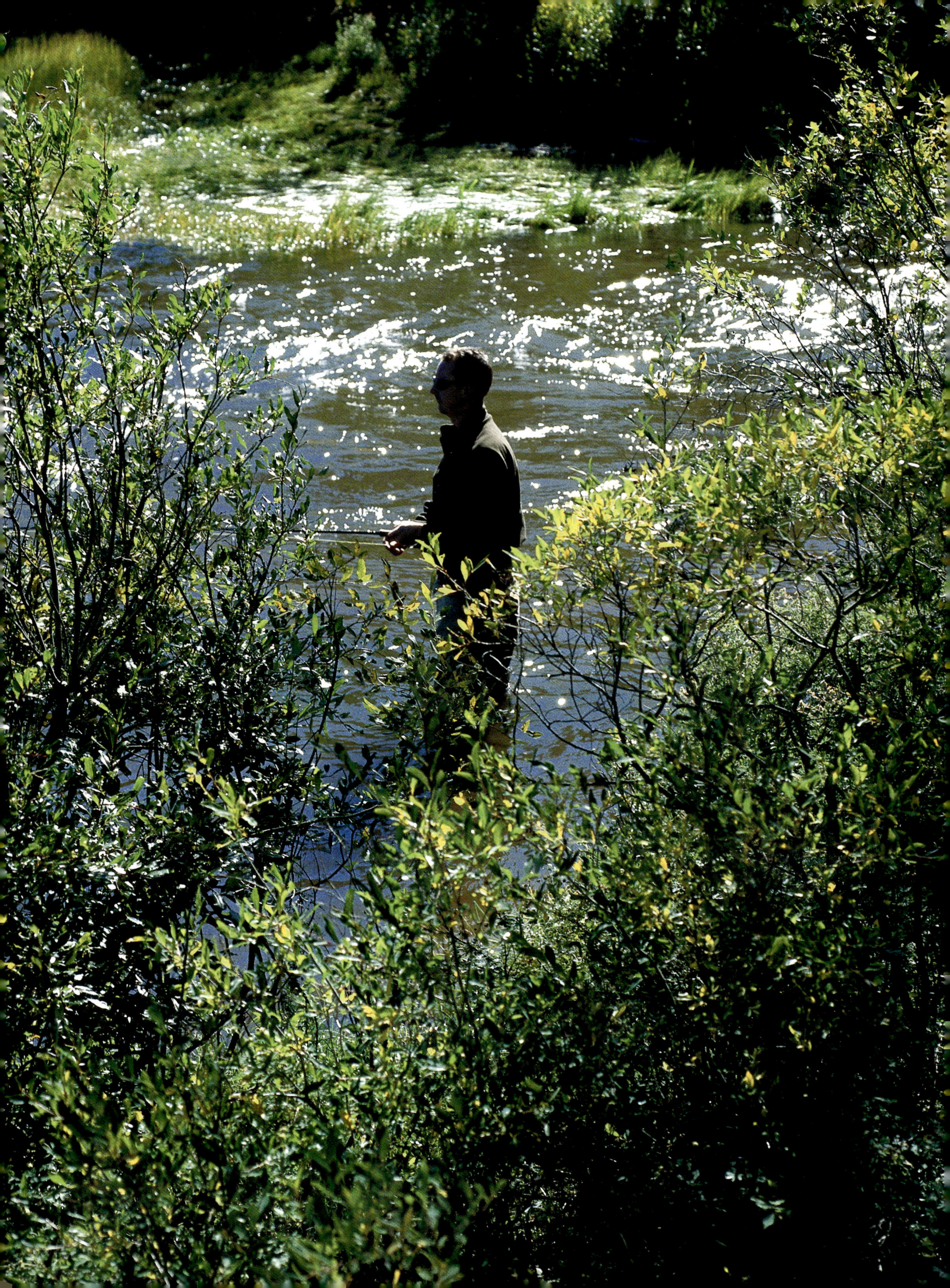

WILD WATERS *A decent breeze helps the fishing on most Irish loughs, whether you're after salmon, sea trout, or wild browns. Dull days are, however, considered vastly superior to bright ones, when the fishing can be notoriously difficult.*

intensified with the first of the savage frosts. Vincent says this is so: "The people of the upper river have always taken salmon, for hundreds of years, up until just 50 or 60 years ago, within my own memory. They called them the Black Salmon, and they would salt them for the winter or eat them fresh for Christmas dinner. They would strap turf to their pikes, douse it in paraffin, set it alight, and blind the fish in the ankle-deep water…" Just imagine: men huddled against the first storms of winter or moving through still, moonlit nights when the fish could be heard exploding in the shallows. The calls of the farmers. Plans shouted across the streams. Cries of exasperation and disappointment. Shouts of triumph, for the men had to win in the end. There could be no real hiding place for the fish, but once the eggs were laid and fertilized then why not take the tired, spent bodies for the benefit of the community? How could God have devised things more neatly?

Kevin Factor owns Glencar House now. He's an American, and if you ask him how he got to Glencar in the first place he looks somewhat puzzled, as though the whole of his present life is a mystery to him! He clearly recognizes and warms to the breathtaking beauty of the land and the spirit of those who live here, but it's a clear-sighted affection: "I must introduce you to Ned; he'll help you no end. Mind you, 99 percent of what he says is bullshit and the rest is lies! You have to realize that the guests, me even, we're only here for the amusement of the staff."

With typical American freshness, Glencar is run on the most egalitarian of principles. When there is water in the valley and the fish are running, all that matters is knowledge of the river, of the lies, and of the habits of the salmon. Then, the visiting banker would swap bank accounts with the local bin-man and the broker would trade his Rolls for the knowledge of the man with holes in his waders. Yes, that's what Kevin likes about the fishing hereabouts. It's the greatest of levellers, and the fish are impressed by nothing but skill.

> "Yes, that's what Kevin likes about the fishing hereabouts. It's the greatest of levellers, and the fish are impressed by nothing but skill."

A WORLD OF HIS OWN (opposite) *This is what fishing is truly about. It's so engrossing that it completely captivates you and clears the mind of any outside thoughts. Fishing is said to be relaxing. Well, that depends what you mean. Fish hard and you'll undoubtedly end the day totally exhausted.*

FISHING GLENCAR

For fly fishing, a single-handed seven- or nine-weight will be adequate – seven for grilse and nine for the bigger springers. There's no need for a double-hander, because access is good and there's no need to wade. The river is actually too rocky and treacherous for that. The season starts in February and in cold weather you should use a sink tip to get flies six to eight feet down in the head of the streams. Use traditional Irish flies – the Lemon and Grey, or shrimp patterns, or Stoat's Tails and Willie Gunns. Cast slightly down stream and let the flies pull across the current. In the slower pools you can back up and try a riffling hitch, although this is more for the grilse in the tails of the pools as the year develops.

For spinning, it was once all about brown and gold Devon Minnows, about two-and-a-half inches long. In cold water, the locals would move to blue and silver. In heavy water, a traditional copper Toby was a killer, because it could get down to the depths and you could retrieve it incredibly slowly. Today, the ubiquitous Flying C is the most used lure on the river. Common colours are black and silver, and black and copper. In dirty water, a yellow body can be good. Work across and down, vary the speed, and cover the water very

BESIDE DANCING STREAMS *The true beauty of Irish fishing is in its wilderness, its ability to offer you riverbanks where the only footprint is your own, with fish that may well never have seen a fly before.*

FISHING UNFETTERED *Keep it simple, keep your gear light, and make your fishing mobile. Ireland possesses thousands of miles of streams like this that you can explore to your heart's content, and the chances are you won't meet another angler all day long.*

carefully. The deeper and heavier the water, the bigger the lure you will want, moving it as slowly as possible near to the bottom.

There are plenty on the river that use the worm, but this is a very rocky water with boulders everywhere, and this rules out lead – you simply get snagged up every cast. Instead, you can use a small sliding pike float set at around four or five feet deep. Put two or three lobworms on a size two and cast them out into the current to let them trot down with the river. Count to 10 after the float disappears and tighten it to the fish. There's no real need to strike, as there is with the shrimp that become legal at the beginning of June. With a shrimp, you can use the same set-up, but you must strike at once. And, as Michael says, sometimes that's too late!

Trolling the lough is popular when the river is low and unfishable. It's a relaxed way of fishing, and it does allow you to appreciate the beauty of the Kerry countryside hereabouts. It's common to use three or four rods so that a strip of water anything up to 30 feet wide is being fished. In the early season, 28-gram Tobies are favourite, but Rapalas also catch a fair share of fish. Thirty-five yards is the optimum distance to work the lures behind the boat so that the Toby works about five feet beneath the surface. A longer or shorter line and the Toby will tend to work higher, above the heads of the salmon. It pays to measure the line out on the land beforehand and mark it with a red stop-knot so it's easily seen when you're out on the water.

Not all Tobies are the same! Try them in the water alongside your boat and watch their action. What you want is a really good fluttering movement. Every now and again, some Tobies pause and then deviate between one and two feet to either side. Michael calls this "the Ali Shuffle", and those Tobies that don't have the action don't catch the same number of fish. Fascinating but true

THE ART OF DAPPING
Mayfly Magic

"The whole art is to let the fly sit on the water and drift ahead of you, in front of the boat."

THE PAST AND THE PRESENT *Although progress has touched Ireland in many ways, echoes of the past still reverberate strongly in its quieter, more remote areas. This scene from Lough Arrow over half a century ago seems equally vibrant today.*

Dapping is simply the concept of using the wind to billow out your line and allow a large natural or artificial fly to skitter on the surface in as natural a way as possible. It's probably the oldest, and certainly the simplest, form of fly fishing, and it dates back centuries. A size 10 hook is the norm, but choose a wide bend pattern to take two natural mayflies if you're fishing the real thing. Some anglers increase this to a size eight or even six! You hook the flies through the thorax and they stay on well. Pick them off the bushes around the shoreline before you start fishing – at the height of the season it's the work of just a few minutes. Telescopic rods are generally favoured, extending to 14 or even 16 feet in length. The good thing about a telescopic rod is that if the wind really rises and the full rod becomes difficult to manage, you can ship down a section and fish with a rod of reduced length.

Centre-pin reels are used all the time, with plenty of 15-pound nylon backing. To this you attach 10 or 12 feet of synthetic floss, and this in turn is attached to a leader, between 4 and 8 feet of 6-pound nylon monofilament. It's unwise to go lighter than this because this is the time you're likely to catch some very big fish indeed. All these measurements can be changed according to the weather conditions, and in a very stiff wind you probably won't need the floss at all. It's only there to help catch the breeze if there isn't much of it about. Equally, you can use a heavier leader if you see some really big browns moving, as very little of it ever actually touches the water at all.

The whole art is to let the fly sit on the water and drift ahead of you, in front of the boat. Lift the fly off from time to time and let it settle again in a natural way. This is the key. Your mayfly has to behave as much like the real thing as you can make it. A single drift on a water the size of Corrib can cover miles, and you will be passing over scores of fish as you go – but it can be frustrating. If you see a good fish move to the right or left of your drift and you're on your own, there is very little you can do except let your fly move directly in front of you. Ideally, you need two people dapping and one on the oars to move the boat after a sighted big fish.

The fish themselves move upwind, and you will see them rising, taking naturals in a very lazy way. Yours is likely to be accepted, providing it doesn't drag or look at all unnatural. The strike is all important – always delay it until the fish has turned down with the fly firmly in its mouth. If you're too quick, you'll simply pull the fly out. A good dapper strikes with an upward stroke of the whole arm. This is particularly important if a long line is being fished.

Mayflies aren't the only insects that can be used on the dap – big sedges and craneflies are probably just as good – and artificials work almost as well. Either let the fly sit quietly on the surface or work it a little by lifting and shaking the rod tip.

The Life Cycle of the Mayfly

Mayflies are truly magnificent creatures, easily the largest of Ireland's up-winged fly species, and they create a stunning picture on these beautiful waters. The mayfly season is real fun time, when armies of anglers set out to go dapping.

The life of the mayfly begins as the egg hatches and the nymph appears. The nymphs live in stones and vegetation and are hunted by the trout. As their time to emerge approaches, they become more active and increasingly vulnerable. They'll even come up to the surface a few times immaturely, and they can be intercepted by the trout as they rise or fall. The critical time comes as they wait in the surface film until their wing cases split open and they emerge as winged flies, or duns, as they must then wait for their wings to dry sufficiently to allow them to fly to the bank.

The dun sheds its skin again, sometimes after several days, to become the spinner – the shining, spiralling, iridescent pinnacle of mayfly life. This is when mating takes place, and the females then return to the water's surface to lay their eggs, which sink to the bottom and eventually hatch out as nymphs. The spinners die soon after the egg-laying process, and are yet again heavily preyed upon when dead or dying.

MAYFLY MADNESS *Ireland has always revelled in the arrival of the mayfly, and the first bloom of these glorious, spiralling insects signals party time along the shores of all the major loughs. The great event is celebrated here in a painting.*

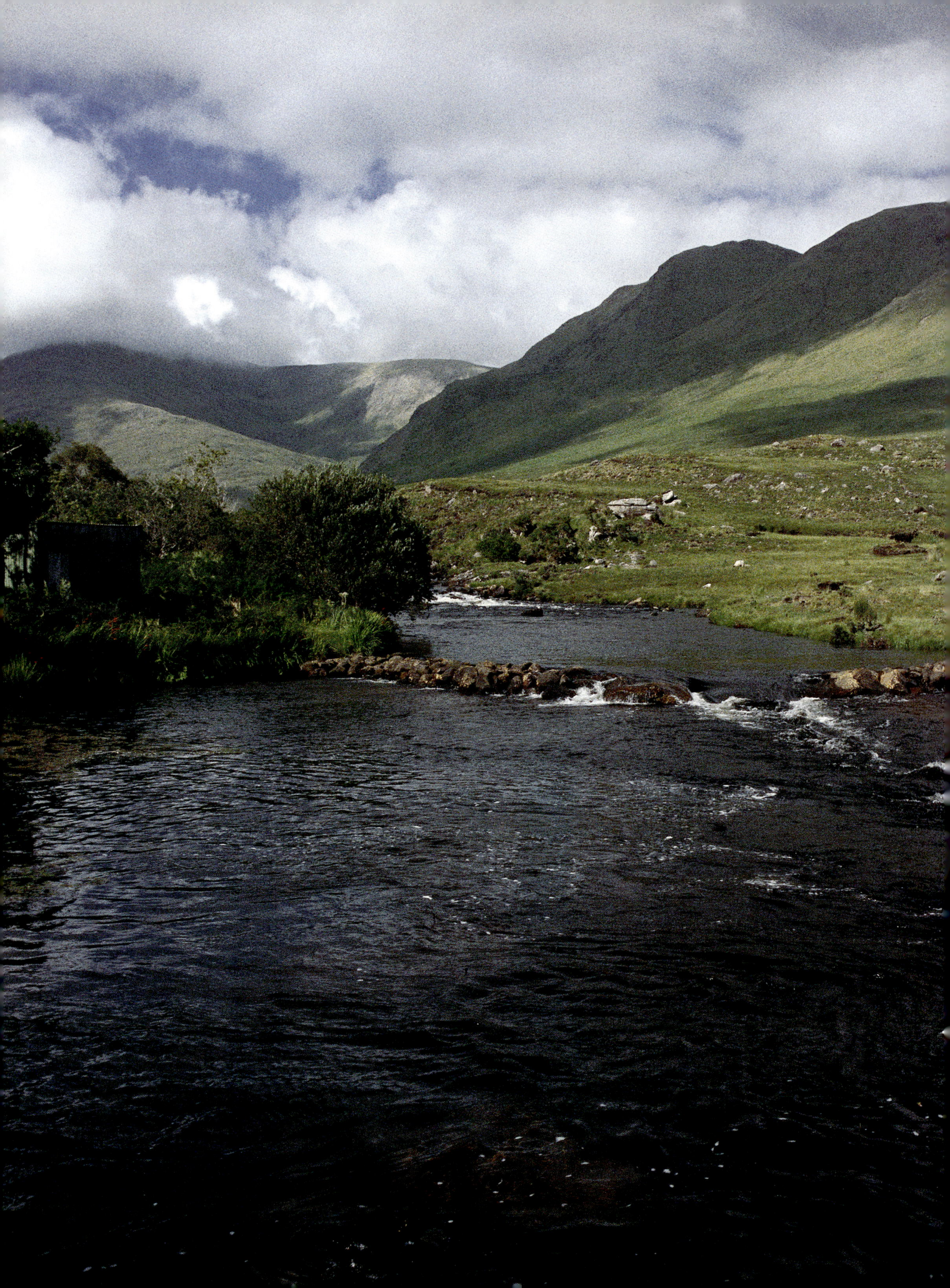

Summer

"Give me a waxing moon, a few wisps of darting cloud, and a river where the sea trout are busy, and I'll show you what I mean about Ireland."

A fly rod in Ireland in the summer – now, truly, this is absolutely as good as it gets, believe me. There are still the remnants of the mayfly around, and you'll find plenty of trout that aren't yet sick of them. And even if they are, don't worry, because there are abundant hatches of just about everything else that swims and flies. After the mayfly glut, you'll find that the browns are simply prime, thick and creamy as butter. They're no longer hungry, so they're wary, and that makes the catching of them even better. Pat yourself on the back if you get three or four out of the Corrib on a hard day. But that's how it should be, isn't it? If you don't ache to land every fish you hook, you shouldn't be putting in the steel in the first place.

And then there are the sea trout – where they can still be found – and they are well and truly on the move. Sea trout scintillate: they bring whole rivers into pulsating, rich-veined life, and those who have contributed to their decline should at the very least be made to put the wrong right. Where there are no longer sea trout, then you'll find ladders of grilse, which are almost as good. Ireland really specializes in fish between three and six pounds, and on the right gear they fight like demons. I don't think I've ever seen as many summer salmon as I have in Ireland: it sometimes looks as though all the world's stocks have come to this one lucky island.

As if all this were not enough, you also have the sea and all the sport that's opening up here for the fly fisherman – the sparkling blue days and galloping white-horse seas, air so pure it blows your mind, and colours so vivid your eyes ache. Find the sea bass in the sheltered coves and you'll wonder how any fish can hit a fly quite that hard. Go for the pollock over the craggy inshore rocks and you'll marvel at their vertical dives to the bowels of the sea. Track the mullet up the estuaries as the tide oozes in, and follow their waving tails as they nosedive to feed. Bone-fishing in the Bahamas may just have the edge, but after a morning's boning you can't then go and fish the dry fly for a Corrib brown!

I've already talked about fishing early and late, and all sport at this time is good, but in Ireland it becomes magical. I've been up at the crack of dawn in a score of countries, but Ireland remains uniquely special. The peace and quiet are certainly total, but it's the light that makes it so wondrous, shifting and wavering until you're holding your breath, wondering exactly what hue will flicker up next. The lough is rich and oily, and the trout delight in heavy, ponderous takes that are all but impossible to miss.

You can then sleep the day out if you choose, waiting for evening to come, the softest evenings you will meet anywhere outside the tropics. Give me a waxing moon, a few wisps of darting cloud, and a river where the sea trout are busy, and I'll show you what I mean about Ireland. Did I say this is as good as it gets? No, it's much, much better than that.

THE CORK BLACKWATER
Blackwater Lodge

"I've always been in the dark with my spey casting. Thank you for showing me the light."

Ian Powell and Glenda, his wife, have revolutionized Blackwater Lodge. The hotel was originally the old railway station – the signal box is still there – and the line itself ran through the present restaurant, but in the 16 years of his ownership, Ian has transformed the Lodge into the most magical of anglers' dens. It's not just that the Blackwater Lodge is comfortable now, with an excellent menu and some superb fishing: it's got what every fishing hotel really needs, and that's a real bar – one where stories, tall and true, are swapped, where information is bartered. This is no problem at Blackwater Lodge, because there are so many beats and they are exchanged so regularly there's no need to hoard knowledge. This is a bar for real fishermen, not the habitués of designer angling hotels, one where the owners are true anglers and not the kind that simply talk a good session in the bar.

QUITE A TEACHER

And, by common consent, anglers don't get much better than Glenda. She's got all the qualifications and certificates, but they're pretty dry testament to what a brilliant teacher she actually is. Ted Keane, a giant of a man, had been coming to Blackwater Lodge for seven years and had always striven to spey cast, but teaching him had proved totally beyond his usual ghillie. Then Glenda took him out to Ballyhooley, made him put down the spinning rod and take up his fly gear, and within the hour he was hitting the far bank with a single spey. That evening there were tears coursing down his face, and later that week a bouquet of flowers appeared with the message, "I've always been in the dark with my spey casting. Thank you for showing me the light."

PASTORAL IDYLL (opposite) *It's easy to call the Blackwater a friend. It's a kind, generous, welcoming sort of river winding through some of Ireland's most mellow landscapes. Stand almost anywhere on its banks and wherever you look you will see the best of rural Ireland.*

LORD OF THE STREAM *Ian Powell is at work on a quite lovely piece of fly water, which he fishes with methodical ease. There's something addictive about the pull of a taking salmon: there are those who find that this particular sensation is actually the peak of all their thrills.*

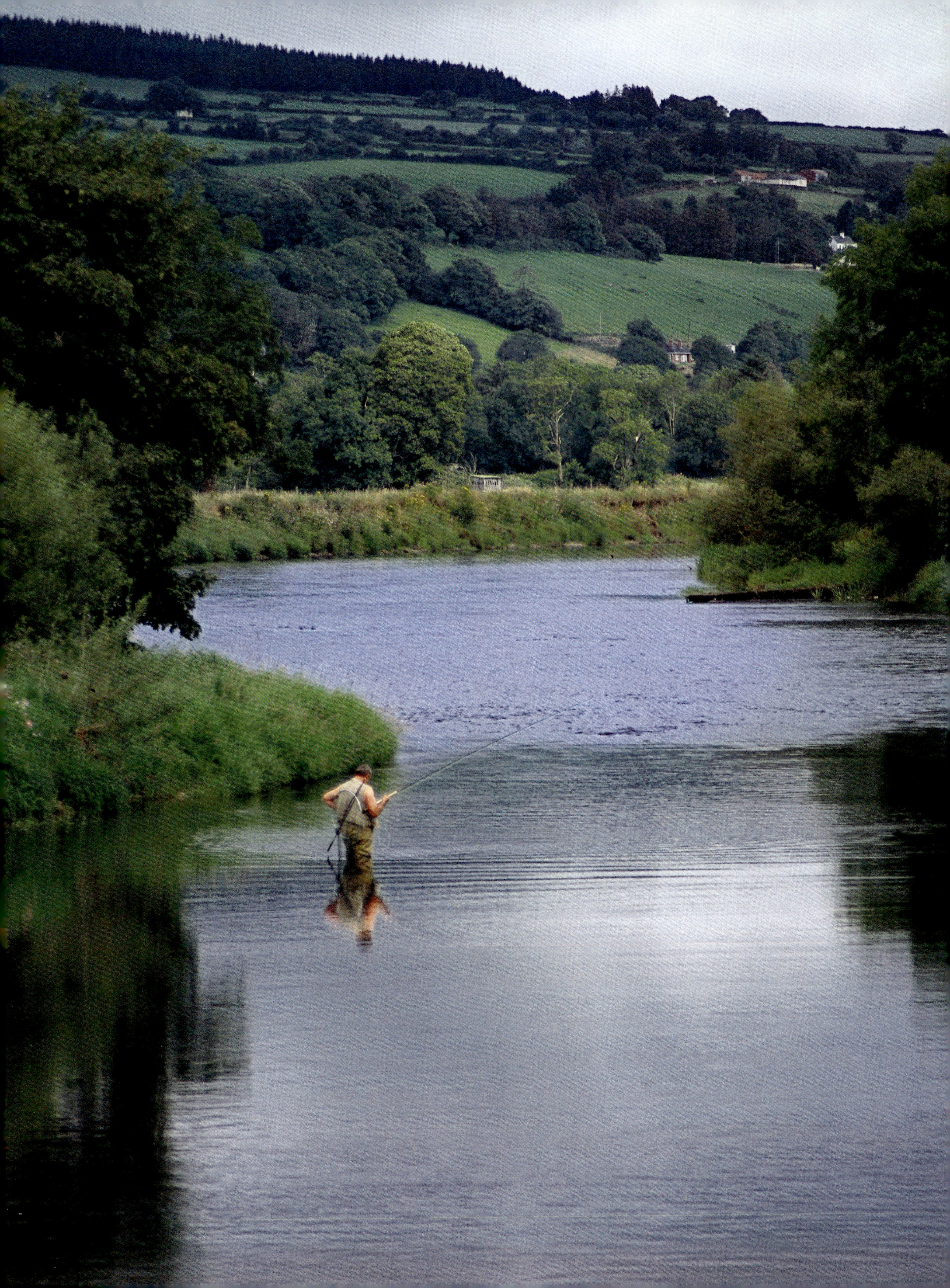

58 The Cork Blackwater

THE WINDING RIVER *The Blackwater meanders its way through the countryside with countless lazy bends, tempting pools, and glorious ripples. And, above all, the salmon still run in pulsating numbers.*

SHADOWS OF THE PAST *Ian and his guests clatter through the Priory as the dusk seeps in and the day's fishing draws to a close. This is a moody, atmospheric end to a fishing session: one that you're glad you haven't prolonged into true darkness.*

This morning the bar is packed as soon as breakfast is over: guests of all nationalities, ghillies, Glenda, children, cooks, aunts, uncles, and cousins, and a right hubbub of joyous expectation. It is decided that I will accompany Ian with two Americans, Kevin and Raymond, who will leave their wives to do the shops in Cork city.

We make our way to the river and look at the first beat that Ian has selected. He doesn't particularly like it – you can always tell when someone really wants to show off their water but isn't quite sure it's up to the mark. No matter. We take off again upstream. That's the beauty of the Blackwater Lodge, with its 16 beats spread over a vast length of river. If the fish are still down at the bottom, Lodge guests can fish there. Then, as fish ascend, you just go with them. The fact that there is so much water lets Ian match the angler to the beat perfectly. He's a man who takes time to assess his guests, both as people and as anglers. With his choice of water, he can put the good fly angler on exactly the right runs for a fine day's sport. Or, if the angler is an out and out wormer and won't be for changing, there are the deep, still pools to suit him. Allocating the beats is a serious job, and Ian waits until all the day's results are brought in, mulled over, and decided upon. He believes everyone should enjoy the day to come... and if you don't enjoy it, then you should be leaving the fish alone.

Fishing Bridgetown Priory

The roads get smaller and more rutted, black-top turns to gravel, and we arrive at Bridgetown Priory. The four of us walk through the ruins, and the Blackwater beyond presents a perfect picture: a long, steady, broken run for Ian to fly fish and, above it, a sumptuous pool steaming with salmon and begging to be spun by the two Americans.

I stick with Ian for the first hour. He is using an intermediate tip to get the fly down nine inches or so below the surface. A size 10 Wilkinson goes on the dropper with a size 12 double Hollow Stoat on the point: he wants a bit more flash than usual, for the river is still peat-stained after continuous heavy rain. A glint in the gloom is vital.

He works the glide expertly: the cast, the mend, the rod out across the stream, the tightest of control at all times. Hawk-like concentration. He paces the fly precisely with his rod tip, and once it reaches dead water it is recast and he moves on down. "Notice how I hold a good two-yard loop of line at the reel. We're a long way upstream here and there are fish here that have been resident for quite a while. They will give a slow, solid pull and it's always best to let them have line before lifting into them. From fresh-run fish you get a quicker, more instant jab."

It's lovely to watch, sitting in the mild air on an untrodden bank, listening to the river, watching the kingfisher, studying Ian's technique. The Blackwater is a relatively big river, but it still retains its intimacy, and it's so varied that it always engages your imagination and interest.

Suddenly, there's a heck of a lot of clamour upriver, around the bend – American voices so excited that I just have to go and take a look. Raymond is playing a fish, but with such ferocity and on such a tight line that the outcome is inevitable. The salmon cartwheels a third time and you know that something's got to give – it's the hook hold that does. Still, never mind. Kevin is absolutely spellbound by two grazing swans, and Raymond has two important questions for me. Firstly, can they both touch the cow that's watching us over the fence and, secondly, what on earth are these little brown mounds of earth that Ian called molehills?

The Community Spirit

The cloud cover makes for an early dusk, and out of the gloom comes a tiny grey leprechaun figure, no more than five feet tall, with long wizard-like hair, a vintage rod, and a wicker creel. The elfin fisher slips between the two giant Americans, looks up and down the river, shrugs, and melts away into the mist and drizzle as though he were never here. I tell Ian about it. "Oh yes, just a trout fisher come to watch the water. They do no harm and upset no-one, and this is a live and let live sort of place."

FISHING THE GLIDE *Working a salmon fly is all about control. Yes, you've got to reach the required distances, but length is of no use whatsoever without positive control.*

It certainly is. Annually, in the middle of August, Ian and the Community Council arrange the two-day Ballyduff salmon festival on a massive amount of water. Ian donates all his water to the festival and makes sure a good number of the other riparian owners do as well. Entry costs 70 Euros, and local anglers flock to it to enjoy some of the best fishing on the river. Back at the hotel at night, I'm told, the festival becomes a big party, such enormous fun that I consider changing my plans and staying on for it. "Are you entering, sir?", one of the ghillies inquires. "Because if you are, I suggest you leave your fly rod at home – there'll be some ironmongery flying about and no mistake." I don't scoff: each year the festival raises over 3,500 Euros, which goes to local projects. One year the local school caretaker was picked to fish for the Irish team in Australia, but couldn't possibly pay for his airfare there. The first day of the festival took care of that. Glenda emphasizes the point. "If you're on a high horse here, you're bound to fall off. We're all part of the community, and if we can fit the locals in, we will. Times they're not fishing, they'll probably take a strimmer down and do a bit of cutting for us. As Ian's told you, we all have to live together here."

Supper is wondrous, although it's taken late: Ian and Glenda both have Herculean amounts of work to do running the hotel, arranging the fishing, and even firing up the smokehouse. We talk about Bridgetown Priory and I mention the intense, almost frightening, atmosphere there as the dusk rolled in. Ian and Glenda catch each other's eye. "I was fishing there myself once, alone, when it got late," she says. "I can tell you I would never, ever dream of repeating the experience. There was nothing tangible, of course, and it was obviously just my imagination working overtime, but the thoughts of all those souls over all those centuries and all the lives that have ended there…" Her voice trails off, and we all give a shudder and set ourselves to planning the following day's fishing. Oh, and Kevin can be overheard telling his quite charming wife that, "Gee honey, these cows are really quite gentle things after all!".

... and Kevin can be overheard telling his quite charming wife that, "Gee honey, these cows are really quite gentle things after all!"

HAWK EYE *The eye of the trout is one of the most efficient of all instruments in nature. The seatrout, for example, is able to target the tiniest midge on the darkest of nights.*

PRAWNING – THE WHYS AND WHEREFORES

The whole issue of using bait – prawns, shrimps, or worms – for salmon is a thorny one. Most people I've met in Ireland would claim that fly fishing is the ultimate in terms of both sport and artistry, and that bait fishing comes a poor second, or even third, behind spinning, but some would disagree. I have to admit that I'd done no prawning before and had never understood it until I watched it being done here on the Blackwater in Ian's dextrous hands. The method is both skilful and immensely exciting. The doubt is one of conservation: an argument goes that prawning should be allowed just for the last hour or so of the day, if the angler wishes and hasn't had any luck whatsoever on fly or spinner. This would give some room for optimism on the dourest day, probably provide the angler with a bit of excitement, and make sure he comes back. After all, successful salmon fisheries depend on beats being taken up. Perhaps if prawning is controlled tightly, it is not altogether a bad thing, and as the fish appear to be only ever hooked in the jaw – the strike is very quick – catch and release is still possible.

For tackle, a 10-ft spinning rod is about right. A fixed-spool reel of 15–20lb line with a weight, hook length, and prawn complete the outfit. The prawns are cooked, preserved with salt, dyed (commonly red or purple), and then mounted on the hook by means of a pin secured with elastic thread.

This is primarily a method for low, clear conditions when the fish are not running but are dour and do little more than look at a fly. And it's not a method for beginners, because it does call for very delicate control. The technique is not unlike fly fishing: the aim is to swing the prawn across the current, keeping it just over the bottom… you often feel the bed, and snagging is frequent over rough ground. You don't work the prawn, but let the current take it down and across, so you do need moderately quick water. You must work the runs quickly, because takes are often instant, ranging from real tugs to the merest rattle, easily mistaken for the rasping of gravel or stones.

It's not a method best fished with a downstream wind, as this pushes a belly in the line and you feel a take too late.

Whatever the wind and flow pattern, you are always mending the line to keep as direct a contact with the bait as you can. Look for the salmon lying in the middle of the river, but examine the crease line between quick and slow water closely. Hold the rod quite high to keep the prawn skipping bottom, and keep your wits about you. The same salmon will often follow a prawn several times, knocking it and, even more frustratingly, sucking the underbelly off the prawn, nipping out the eggs. It often helps to trim the little bits of elastic thread, as even these can be nipped and tugged.

Standing at Ian's shoulder, watching him work the prawn with exquisite delicacy, I can see why those who criticize it frequently haven't tried it. A salmon follows his prawn six times, leaving the current, hitting it almost at the near bank in totally slack water – exciting stuff at such close range. We can both see the line flick as the salmon mumbles on the bait. Ian has the line crooked over his finger, watching intently. Of course, in the slack water the salmon has all the time in the world to make its mind up. Ping, pluck, gone. Perhaps if it had been a fresher fish… Ian muses.

THE WONDER BAITS *It seems hardly possible that a change of colour from red to purple should make such an extraordinary difference to whether a salmon takes or not, but it does. There remain mysteries in angling, thank God, and we can be absolutely sure that there are many, many more that still lie undiscovered.*

LOST LIMERICK
Mulcair and Shannon

"... you'll realize that an untouched Ireland can still be found, and that the rural heart of Ireland still beats."

TIMELESS TRADITIONS *The bond between angler and guide goes back decades. The job of ghillying has always provided work and a profession with status and respect.*

STILL MIGHTY (opposite) *The Shannon may have been partially tamed, but it's still a magnificent, pulsating torrent of water. Perhaps the monsters of yesteryear no longer climb its fall but, if you believe Mick, there are still magnificent fish to be found.*

The Limerick ring road at rush hour demonstrates perfectly the horrors of modern Europe – fast food bars, chain hotels, and the rest – and you could be led to think that Ireland has lost the plot, lost what made it special. Surely we, the tourists, are drawn to Ireland by its timelessness and for the unique experience of fishing from another century with all of today's advantages. Well, meet up with Richard and Eleanor Keays just a few miles outside the city and you'll realize that an untouched Ireland can still be found, and that the rural heart of Ireland still beats.

It's a late summer evening, and when you turn off the N24 into the maze of lanes that leads eventually to Millbank House you feel the excitement rising as the green fields slip by and the world becomes quieter and more hushed. It's a golden sunset, and the house and driveway look very fine, both given an air of dignity by the magnificent weeping ash that dominates the grounds.

The house, built in 1733, is the second Keays' family home to stand here. The two buildings have been home to eight generations of the family, and throughout all that time the Keays have been farmers first and foremost, with other occupations bolted on to boost prosperity. Just outside the driveway stand the vestiges of a flax mill that once served the family so well. It's possible to see the remains of the small ponds where the flax was cured, and the waterfall that once drove the mill. A century ago, draining schemes sabotaged the flow and the mill gradually fell into dereliction.

FISHING PROVES THE VITAL ELEMENT

Now it is fishing tourism that helps prop up the farm. When Richard was a lad, there was pressure on him to go onto the land, but times change: 120 acres of land is not a great deal to rely upon, and by the early 1980s the noose had begun to tighten around Millbank Farm as milk quotas sent prices tumbling. Richard and Eleanor have three sons and two daughters, all of whom would like to farm, but in today's climate they have to be discouraged, pushed towards qualifications and, most probably, out of the rural life that they've been brought up in and love.

So it's fortunate that in 1968 the Keays began their guesthouse business and made an early impression in the fledgling tourist market. As Richard says, 30 years ago they were one of only two farmhouses between Rosslare and Limerick offering accommodation, and they were full every night of the season.

Millbank has the feel of a happy house, but it has always survived on hard work. Yesterday, for example, Richard was up very late looking after his guests – mostly French and Swiss. This morning, very early, I had my usual run around the green, dew-drenched lanes of the neighbourhood. As I jogged past the Keays' cattle shed, I

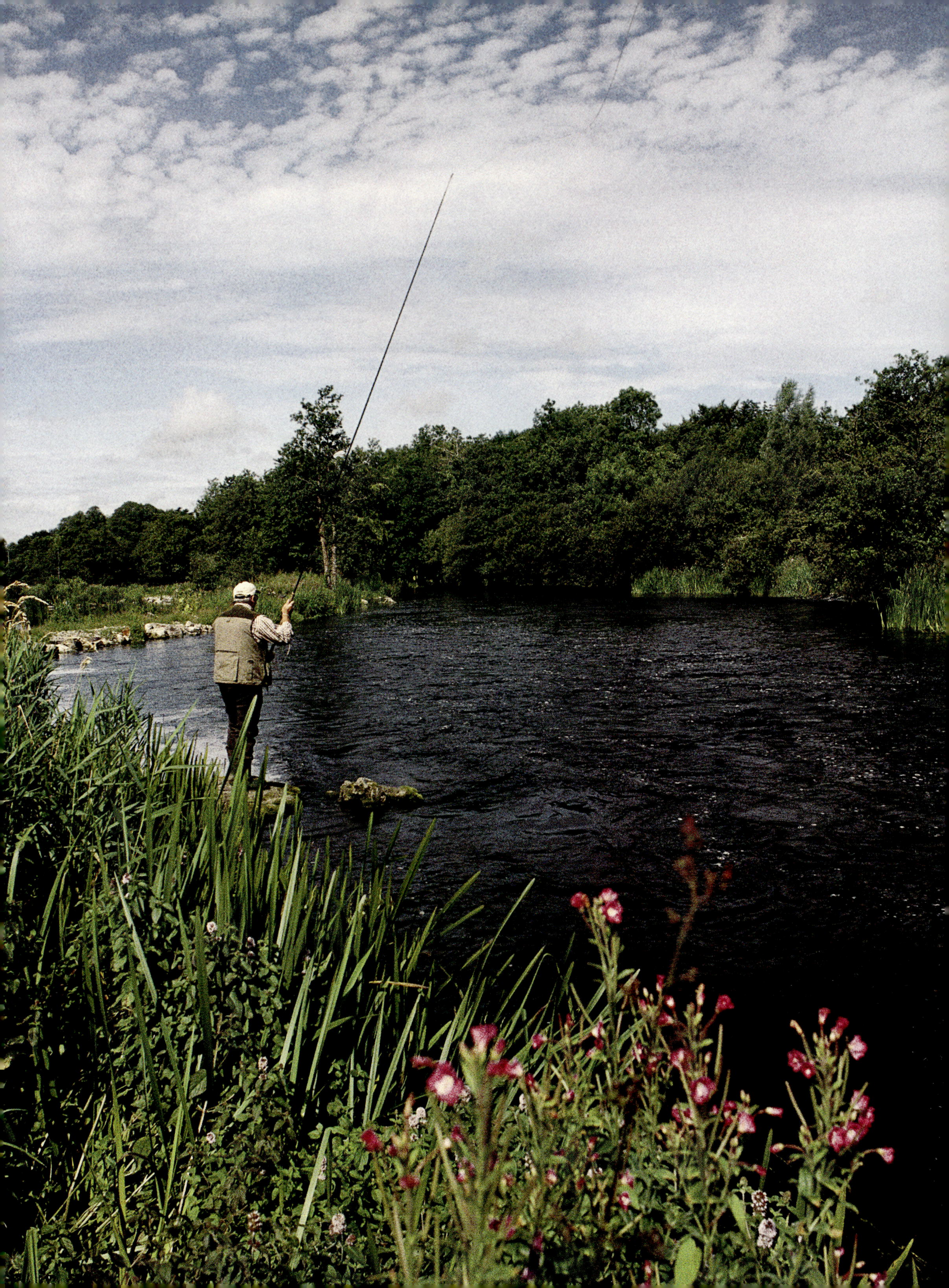

AS IT ONCE WAS *In a word, frightening. The untamed Shannon at Castleconnell a century ago was a piece of water any angler would hold in simple, unadulterated awe. You can see from this photograph why it just had to be fished from boats, but we can only guess at the titanic struggle a 40-pound salmon would inflict in such a torrent.*

FAIRY DELL *This is the Mulcair, the most charming of streams, twinkling through dingles and dells, every inch singing of magic and delights to be discovered. You probably won't see a soul. It's as though the river belongs to you and the spirits of the forest.*

could hear Richard whistling at his work. He'd been up since a quarter to five. So what's new, he seemed to shrug to me, when I commented on the fact later: life's never been a doddle hereabouts. He remembers back to childhood when each and every pupil had to bring a sod of turf for the fire to school in the morning. The eleven o'clock break wouldn't be spent playing in the yard, polishing up the slide or dodging the snowballs. Rather, the kids would be sent to collect tinder for the next morning's fire. Lunch would be bread and jam, and tea poured from old lemonade bottles stoppered with a cork of newspaper folded into the top. Half an hour before lunch all the bottles were put by the stove to heat, a monitor appointed to shuffle them.

Not for a moment would Richard ever complain about a childhood that he has always regarded as rich and fulfilling: and because the Mulcair river runs through the Millbank land, Richard always had his fishing and was an angler as a toddler. At six years old, he became a member of the Mulcair Anglers' Association and was apprenticed to a fanatical lady salmon angler who used to collect him from school in her motorcar. This was not quite as altruistic as one might think: Richard remembers that there were only two prime fishing positions upon the river. He would be installed on one of them, a dramatic-looking rock, while she fished the other fully out, at which point a swap could be made. When the then equally obsessive doctor knocked off at 3pm, he would, of course, find the two positions fully occupied!

Millbank is full during my stay, and Richard and Eleanor, with repeated apologies, show me to the smallest room in the house. Next door is the children's room, and later that night, lying in bed looking out on the weeping ash, I hear them whispering and giggling in the darkness. When Richard was a child there were 10 who lived in the house, and tonight it seems to me that the ghosts of his past are coming to play. I certainly can't sleep, but that's not surprising: tomorrow morning, you see, I am off a few miles to the Shannon at Castleconnell, once the most famous stretch of salmon river in the whole world.

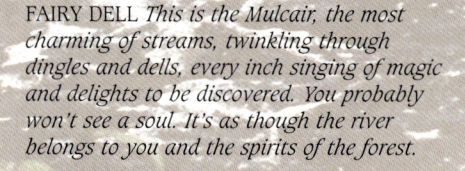

The Magic of Castleconnell

In the 1940s, hydroelectric schemes tamed the River Shannon above Castleconnell to some degree, and although the river here today is still absolutely magnificent, it was once awesome. This is how Joseph Adams described it in 1924: "The Castleconnell salmon fishing at Limerick is renowned, not only for its huge salmon, but also for the unique characteristics of the river. It is little more than a series of rapids, interrupted with irregular cataracts, which leap and roar, making the water like a thing possessed. The Shannon from Killaloe moves with a sluggish and uneventful flow for about eight miles. Nothing disturbs the dignity of its broad expanse save a dip here and there in its bed, or the west wind, which suddenly sweeps down from the mountains and, with its rough caresses, breaks the placid surface into white-crested waves.

"At the little village that bears the name of the famous fishery, the river, as if too long pent up, throws off all restraint. For about three miles it churns and foams, casting its spray in showers that keep the rocks dripping and clothe its banks and islets in perpetual green.

"It is in this rough water that salmo salar likes to make his resting place, catching the spirit of its unlicensed flood, and poising in its rapids, conscious of a strength that defies its rude violence to beat him back. Here, too, he shows his superiority to all the barriers placed in his way, shooting its rapids like a silver missile projected from a submerged engine, and clearing with a bound its ledges of rock, over which in seething volumes its waters hiss and roar."

"It is in this rough water that salmo salar likes to make his resting place, catching the spirit of its unlicensed flood..."

TO STIR THE SOUL *Who could resist a piece of salmon river as magnificent as this? This is water that simply shrieks to be fished. Although perhaps not what it once was, Castleconnell still offers fishing beyond the dreams of most of us.*

AWESOME *Even in rigid death, fish like this are to be wondered at, but just imagine them in the water – vast, flickering, silver shapes, vibrating with power and purpose.*

SUMMER SALMON *A fresh-run grilse is a fish to be marvelled at, with its subtle hues of silver and pewter, and indescribable tints of oranges and blues.*

The fish certainly reflected their environment. They were short and bull-shouldered, and reached extravagant weights. In *The Salmon Rivers of Ireland* (1913), Augustus Grimble speaks of huge catches, huge specimens, and huge averages. How about Captain Vansittart's catch of 104 salmon weighing in at 2,234 pounds, giving an extraordinary average of 21 pounds plus? Thirty-pounders were run of the mill, and 40-pounders came along with regularity. Fishing was done from cots, or boats, and the angler would fish one piece of water before his ghillie dropped him down to tackle the next, and so on until the beats were fished out. The cot men achieved legendary status: Messrs Tuohy, Scaife, and Williams were men of vast skill, knowledge, and very definite ideas about how fishing should be done. It was widely accepted that you didn't mess with a cot man of standing.

BIG RODS, BIG FLIES

You certainly had to have the right tackle for such big fish in such a cascade of water, and the local firm of Enright's produced tailor-made weapons from its factory in the village. Huge flies, too, were needed in a flood like this, and they were generally tied to 6/0s, hand-forged, specially designed to marry with the vast 21-ft greenheart rods: if anything were to give, it would be the angler, the line or the fish! Hi Regan described Castleconnell salmon flies in 1900: "The salmon flies vary exceedingly and some are remarkable for their great sizes and splendour. Some Indian Crow, the brightest silks, and from six to 12 toppings make up a common gaudy yet harmonious fly. Colour and all you can of it are the points in common which good fly fishers there (at Castleconnell) think well of. Size, glitter, and colour are the real needs."

CASTLECONNELL STATION
The station is still there, a brilliant white beacon to that golden age. Don't you wonder at the number of excited alightings made on that platform and how many dreams were to be fulfilled?

Salmon were the key to the Castleconnell economy in the 19th century. The fishery supported not only Enright's and any number of cot men, but also eight angling hotels, plus the staff on the railway that brought anglers direct from London. There was a special train laid on during the mayfly season.

There's plenty of history cloaking Castleconnell's shoulders. For example, go into the corner store that was once part of the Enright empire and look up at the salmon hanging there. Badly stuffed it may be, but its size is jaw dropping! You must also visit P. J. Guering's bar. You'll marvel at everything Patrick has to tell you about the past, the present, and his plans for the future of Castleconnell fishery. Look, too, at his relics from the great days, and at hooks you'd think were designed for shark, not salmon. This is where the news is spread, where plans are hatched, and in Patrick's tackle den behind the bar you'll find anything you're likely to need for the Shannon here... including a 1950s' Seagull engine that's never been taken out of its box!

Richard has arranged my day with Mick Doherty, a man who has fished Castleconnell for 30 years. We agree I'm in safe hands. Mick is fascinated by big fish – it's impossible to be a part of the Castleconnell scene and not be. "You've seen that 45-pounder in Lee's shop, and prints of salmon near 60 pounds in the bars, so you know what the fishery was capable of. The best I've seen on the bank is just under 30 pounds, but there are always rumours. This season, there were stories flying up and down the river of a 37-pound three-ounce fish taken in June. Everyone agreed that it was a rod-caught fish, but the body disappeared, along with the name of the captor and all the details. Shrimp-caught perhaps, and therefore illegal. Who knows? The point is that the fish itself was genuine. The Shannon can still produce giants."

THE HOME RIVER *Richard Keays, at home on the river that he has known his life long and loves with a passion that isn't hard to understand. Some men like to travel for their fishing. Others, more lucky, recognize that they have already found their Paradise.*

FISHING CASTLECONNELL

Mick knows his river, for sure. "The best of all weathers is cloudy, with a really strong south-westerly gusting force six or even seven. This blows straight up the river and tends to push the fish out of the deeps, especially on beat eight. Then they lie up on the shallows – we say it stirs 'em up. Even if it's hardly possible to cast, providing you can get a fly out you stand a great chance.

"We're in the middle of a difficult summer now. It's low and bright, and there've been fish in since June just waiting to spawn, hanging about, watching and learning. The best, and probably only, approach is to fish hard very early in the morning – the first hour in fact – and then leave the beat all the rest of the day and tackle it again the last hour in the evening. That way it's just possible a fish will make a mistake. Fishing beats like this really does call for cunning: for example, if you're with a friend, you fly fish it down first and he can follow you along afterwards with a worm. But take great care over everything you do."

We walk the river. It's a glorious day for a tourist, with fluffy, white clouds high in a blue sky that spells disaster for the fisherman. It doesn't matter to me, drinking in the flow of his words. "See the 'V' in the rocks of the weir?" he says. "Come back in June and every few minutes you'll hear the thump of climbing salmon as they pour through it. Now, see that pyramid-shaped rock, that's the one above the alder? Salmon go straight there to lie up, and then they zigzag across the river to that far rock. Yes, that's the one, and that's another place they're vulnerable. Once you get to know Castleconnell, you improve your chance of picking the best beat for any particular day. Beat six is straight and quick, and this is a cracker when fish are running through fast. The other beats, eight especially, all bend with deep pools and are excellent for holding fish. You've got to think about what the river offers and what the fish will be doing.

"The water is so crystal clear that you can see the salmon coming to the fly. Let's say you've had a hard week and this is your first chance. And let's add to it the fact that this might be a big salmon, bigger than you've ever seen before. You don't want to mess up. So, watch it and wait until it turns – only then lift the rod, and not before. In deep water, you'll often feel a thump and see the line tightening. Hit it immediately. Often the mistake is to wait until you feel the take in slow water. If you delay, chances are the fish will be gone. Sometimes the salmon's just too excited itself, and it will hit so eagerly that it will miss. But don't despair. There are times a salmon will come three or four times and you'll get him in the end. A lot of the old lads will just sit down if they miss a fish and have a chat and a cigarette, and when they try again the fish will be really up for it. Fresh fish are much more forceful, whereas fish like we've got today will be much harder to tempt. In fact, you know, while the sun's up like this, I just don't see the point much in struggling on. What we could do is come back at last knockings and try then with a bit more chance. In the meanwhile, we could drop down the River Mulcair, where I know there's a lot of trout to be had."

HUMBLE HOME OF DREAMS Fishing huts hold a special place in the affections of all anglers. Old, fusty, and a-ripple with spider's webs, they are monuments to piscatorial history, places where you can almost touch the passions and the excitement that have filled them. A hut does not exist that doesn't have a thousand tales to tell.

Brown Trout at Mulcair

In terms of miles, the Mulcair river is not far from Castleconnell, but to find my way back to the delightful stretches of river that Mick introduced me to would be way beyond my navigational skills. Endless tiny green lanes, overhung by trees, skirted by fields and farmhouses, led us here and there to a lost land. The Mulcair is an absolute delight, and although it hosts good salmon runs from time to time, it is definitely the wild browns that we believe will save our day.

Decisions, decisions. Mick shakes his head and rummages through box after box of flies. "It will get easier late," he says. "The bigger fish will be up around about dusk when the sedges are out. Still, 'tis a grand, soft day and I'm not doubting we'll be catching some fish." He attaches a small Olive to the point with a light Hare's Ear on the dropper so that he can fish the two flies in the surface zone. Everything is light and tight, with short casts dead straight across the river. He lets the two flies swing downstream a rod's length or two before arrowing them over the river again. Mick is constantly on the move, seeking out new pieces of water and rising fish. "Do you know how much it costs to fish this river?" he asks. "Twelve euros! Twelve euros for miles and miles and miles of it. No, that's not for the day – it's for the year!"

Mick catches fish, not especially large, but spanking wild browns. They skitter here and there, and even 8-ounce fish welly their way downriver. "I could go heavier," he muses. "Goldheads and heavier nymphs fish deeper, so you cast them upstream to get them down, bouncing the bottom. The true wet fly is different. You fish them down and across, very near the surface. Always on a short line, searching behind boulders, in amongst tree roots and snags. It's a really inquisitive form of fishing. You need chest waders or thigh boots to get close to the fish. Small, quick browns and long lines aren't a good combination at all."

Watching Mick fish, you appreciate instantly not just his energy and casting efficiency but also his speed in reacting to any take. His eyes never stray from his tippet. Anything is struck at – a zip forward, a snatch in the current, or a brief hold against the stream. If a trout dimples where the Olive might be riding, then the rod flicks up and the fish is invariably on.

We walk for miles, across fields, through woods, past the ruins of mills, barns, houses, and ancient fortifications. We see all manner of birds, a fox, and the spraints of otters. The further we walk, the better the fishing becomes. The valley narrows and the river is totally crowded in with trees, so it's like looking down a long, black tunnel. It is here that some of the best browns on the Mulcair are resident. We hear them slooping and clooping away in the gloom, calling out for us to return another day.

Tonight, again, I find it hard to sleep. The images of the Shannon at Castleconnell still cascade through my mind. How would I react if one of those 30-pounders should swirl over my fly and the line begin to tighten? Would I fluff it, or take my chance? Would my dreams be fulfilled, or would they melt like snowflakes in the sea?

ANOTHER WORLD *Paddy's Bar and Tackle Shop convince you there is still magic aplenty left in Ireland. There is nowhere else like it in the whole of Europe. You leave it rubbing your eyes and barely believing what you've just experienced. Do go there if you can.*

THE FUTURE *Tiny and perfectly formed, the Mulcair's trout and salmon parr are the promise for the years to come. Treat them carefully. They are our future.*

BATTLES WITH MONSTERS

So your great fish is there on the end of your thrumming line. What now? How do you maximize your chances of landing it? Well, first of all, try to avoid being seen by the fish for as long as possible. On first being hooked, very many big fish of all species will not immediately realize there is danger. The pressure on them is unnatural, but they don't always associate it with danger, and they're likely to come close to the bank or the boat with little opposition. Once they see the angler or the boat, that's when the fireworks are likely to start. This is very important in the final stages of the battle, because it's surprising how many fish can summon up the energy for a last rush if the sight of a looming angler alarms them.

Keep calm. Keep calm and don't panic. If you lose your head you will lose your fish. Be positive. Aim to assert yourself from

FISH ON *The strike is made, the line zips tight, and the rod keels over. Brown trout, or grilse, or big salmon? The screaming reel will soon tell the tale, and you had better be ready.*

AN EXCITEMENT HARD TO BEAR *This is it, the moment we all wait for with such high hopes. A fine, wild, brown trout fins to the surface, its mind set on sucking in an artificial from the surface film. Let the battle commence.*

the moment the fight begins. Often it's a good idea to walk a fish away from danger. Simply hold the rod at right angles to the river and walk smoothly, slowly, and steadily up the bank. The chances are that the fish will follow. Walking a fish also builds the angler's confidence and somehow demoralizes the fish… don't ask me how, but it works. Always make a fish work hard for every yard of line that it takes from you. It's vital to know how and when to put the pressure on a fish. During a run, you will begin to sense that the fish is slowing down and perhaps tiring. At this point, begin to increase the pressure noticeably. If the fish rises in the water and splashes on the surface, keep the rod low because it's a dangerous moment. Anglers who aren't positive play fish with rods only half bent, and the length of the battle is increased immensely. This does the fish no good and the chances of a hook pulling free are all the greater.

Pumping is an invaluable technique. A big fish that settles out in mid-stream where the water is quick and deep is a serious problem. As soon as a big fish feels immovable, start pumping. Take hold of the rod around about the first eye and pull slowly but firmly upwards. As soon as your rod is vertical, or even a little over your shoulder, wind in as you lower the tip towards the water. Repeat this process as often as you can, and you will find that the big fish moves towards you gently, hardly aware of what is going on.

Be aware. Keep your eyes wide open during the fight and keep looking for potential snags that could prove dangerous in the later stages of the fight. Try to be aware of patches of slack water where you might position a boat or where you might try to lead a fish. Look for any sandy, shelving landing areas that you can begin to make for when the fight looks to be drifting towards its end.

As for the landing, don't chase a fish with the landing net, but draw the fish towards it, over it, and then lift. If the water is shallow, simply lead the fish into the edge until it beaches. You can then guide it half out of the water, free the hook, take your quick photograph, and let it swim away again.

Always have complete confidence in your tackle, and make sure that it is just as good as you can get it. Be certain that you have enough line on, and that the line is of adequate breaking strain. Have confidence in your knots, but double check them just to be sure. Check even the mesh of your landing net: I once had a 35-pound-plus pike fall through the bottom of an old landing net and, believe me, that caused problems!

IRRESISTIBLE *To watch a salmon fly in the water makes sense of the whole question of the take. Worked properly, the flow of the current brushes liquid, lifelike movement into the fly. It hovers and twitches and falls and rises in a way that shrieks out "take me".*

MICK'S ADVICE FOR CASTLECONNELL

After 30 years at Castleconnell, Mick is regarded as one of the gems on this piece of the river, and his words of advice are pearls:

Always wear polarizing glasses. The safety issue is an important one, but also the water is incredibly clear these days, possibly due to the appearance of zebra mussels in the system. These are filter feeders and, although the water used to be quite murky, now it's always like gin.

ZEBRA MUSSEL

You will probably need a 14-ft rod in spring to get the best out of the water, but in summer you can scale down to a 12- or even 10-ft rod and still be able to cover pretty well everything.

In spring you'll need an intermediate or slow-sink line, but in summer a floating line is best for most of the situations you will find.

Much bigger flies were used when the fish were massive and the water had a taint to it. Now, in these clearer conditions, use smaller flies, generally between size 6 and 14. The Black Goldfinch is the most famous, but also try the Hairy Mary, the Garry Dog, and a close relative, the Michelangelo. Leaders should be between 9 and 10 feet, and 14-lb breaking strain is about right in the spring, but drop as low as 8 in the summer.

Cast at 45 degrees downstream and really work the fly across, using the rod to impart life. Mark any fish that moves, and cover it as soon as possible. If you don't raise a fish that you've sighted, then leave him and go back to him later. If you raise a fish and miss it, give him time to recover a little and then try again.

LOUGH CURRANE
The Sea Trout of Kerry

"... sea trout are probably the most magnificent of all the salmonid species"

WILD DAYS (opposite) *Never for a moment think that any week on the west coast of Ireland will be all balmy, sun-scorched days. There are bound to be depressions like this one marching in from the Atlantic, when the world turns grey and the water becomes a cauldron. But, then, battling the elements is all part of the Irish fishing scene.*

SMILES ALL ROUND *Charlie Chaplin, the world's great entertainer, always found peace down in Kerry where he could fish, relax, and stroll with his family. The Butler Arms was his spiritual oasis.*

This book will more than pay for itself if you take this one piece of advice: if you're negotiating the Ring of Kerry anytime between June and September, then don't think of driving after 10am. It is a road that is bewitchingly beautiful, but there isn't a coach operator in the world that doesn't know it. Travel in the daytime and you can forget any gears but first and second, but travel as the sun is rising, when the most indescribable shafts of light dazzle over the sea, and you will revel in a landscape that is unsurpassed. Choose the right morning and be prepared to have your life changed! A similar claim can be made for the sea-trout fishing on Lough Currane, inland of Waterville on the westernmost limits of Kerry itself.

THE WEALTH OF LOUGH CURRANE

The day I made my entry to Waterville was as wild and wicked as Ireland can muster. It made a nonsense of the word summer. The sea, hundreds of feet beneath the winding road, was a cauldron. Birds were being tossed in the air, and a burst of sleet rattled across the windscreen. It was elemental all right, but perhaps appropriately so: sea trout are probably the most magnificent of all the salmonid species and, in Ireland at least, Lough Currane is their spiritual home. Biologically, sea trout are nothing but browns gone to sea to feed and then returning to fresh water to spawn, but such a

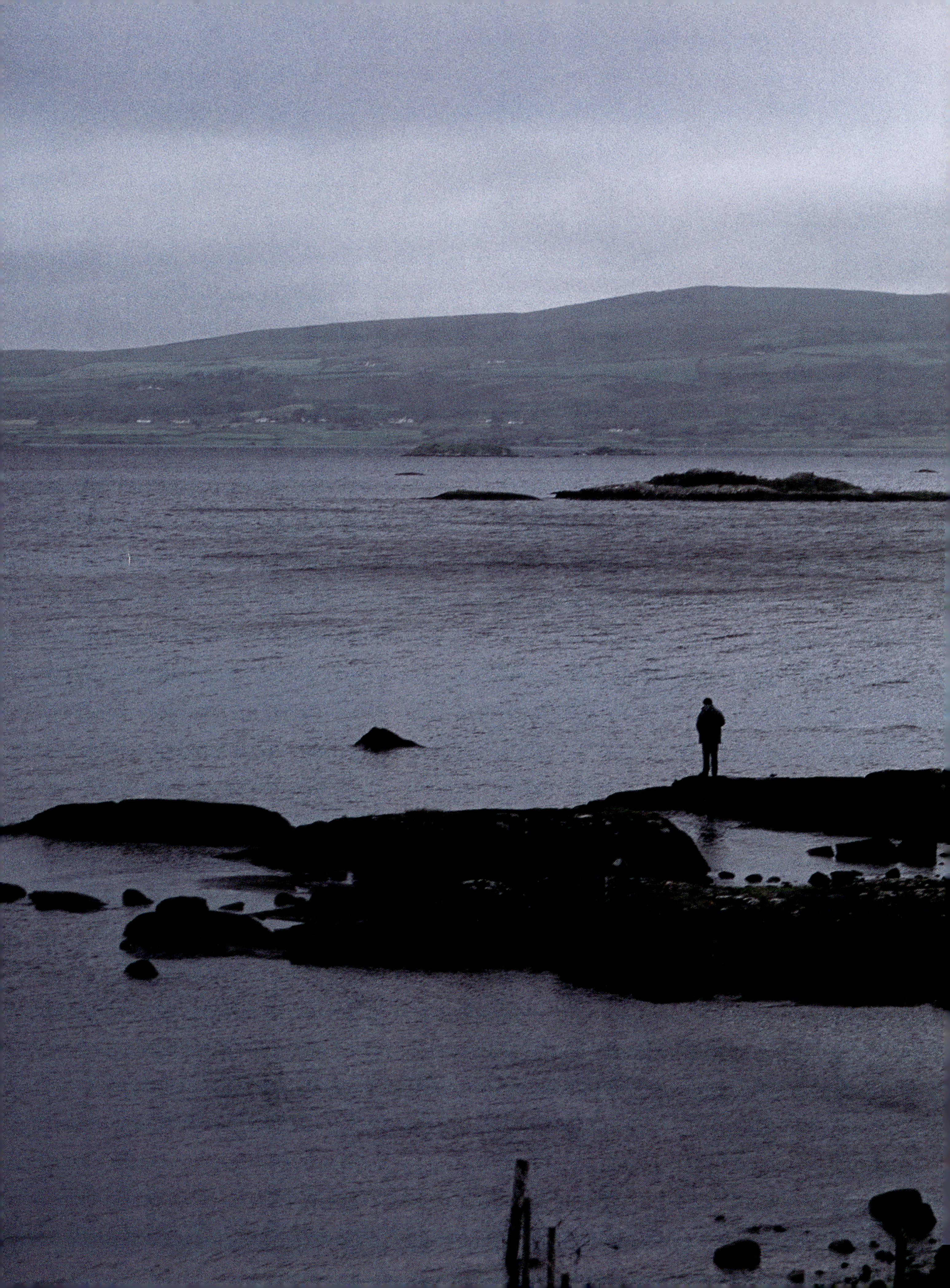

A TROUT FISHERMAN'S ARMADA *Neil O'Shea prepares his boat for the coming day. The guides have their well-rehearsed routine, learnt over generations, skills passed down from their forefathers. You can safely trust them with your very life.*

prosaic description does them no justice at all. There's mystery and magic attached to the sea trout: wandering the ocean, riding the tides, the gypsy fish with the stars in its eyes. The less discerning angler will gush over salmon, but the connoisseur appreciates the sea trout.

At least that's what Neil O'Shea thinks. I meet him in the comfortable residents' lounge of the Butler Arms Hotel, here in Waterville. It is only mid-afternoon, but there's a fire crackling in the grate as the rain streams down the windowpanes. It's so rough that not even Neil has been able to take clients out today, and here is a guide who probably knows Currane better than any other man currently on the lough.

"Oh, I know Currane all right. It's not unusual for me to ghillie out there 40 days in a row, until bad weather like this comes along. You could certainly say I inherited my job. My great grandfather was a ghillie. Both my grandfathers did it, and my father, too. I've got two uncles ghillying, and my sisters have sons who are taking up the trade. Just imagine the huge amount of handed-down knowledge between us all. It's a tradition we're proud of. You could call us a dynasty."

Currane has had its highs and lows, but at the moment sport is sensational, and it's proving a magnificent year for sea trout. There are 15 full-time guides in the village, and they can barely keep up with demand. All these men are driven hard by the fishing, but they work even more diligently to promote the fish themselves. No-one knows quite why the sea-trout fishing in Currane is as magnificent as it is, but in part it's down to the efforts of the ghillies and the local organizations in rearing and transplanting fingerlings and keeping the spawning streams clean and ready for running, ripe fish. Sea trout here are seen as a blessed resource, a gift that is not going to be squandered.

What is in no doubt is that Currane sea trout are both prolific and enormous. In Ireland, the specimen weight for sea trout is set at six pounds: if you look at the lists, you'll see that 99 percent come from the Lough. Seven- and eight-pounders are not unusual. In 1914, a 14-pounder was recorded. Quite why Currane sea trout are this way is not exactly proven. It's possibly something to do with genetics. It's probably something to do with the rich feeding in the sea hereabouts, and the Waterville fish farms deserve some credit, too. New management structures have led to the best lice management protocols in Europe. In 2001, for example, there were hardly any lice to stop the sea trout passing in and out between sea and fresh water, and this is vital. A specimen sea trout is aged anything between six and nine years, and it spawns three, four, or even more times, so fish longevity is central to the success of any sea-trout fishery. The simple bottom line is that when you look at any type of fishing there's got to be a best place, and Lough Currane is it for sea trout.

UNBEATABLE FISHING

Coffee is brought and Neil pours a cup and sits back. "It's easy for the trout to get in from the sea because the river to the lough is only 600 yards long. There used to be a trap there so that the big fish couldn't get through, but for the last 15 or 20 years it's been gone, and the specimens are back. Currane is a big lake in itself – two-and-a-half thousand acres – but there are five other privately owned lakes above it. Many fish stay in the biggest lake, but if there's a lot of water, some fish will just run and run right through the system. The upper lakes tend to fish better late in the season, as spawning approaches, but there are big fish around throughout most of the year. Our average, so far, is between two and two-and-a-half pounds, and that takes into account July and August, when there are lots of juniors about.

"You can tell how long a fish has been in from the sea just by the way it fights. They all fight hard, but fresh fish tend to be high in the water and leap a lot. Staler fish, and bigger ones, keep deep and it's hard to raise their heads up. Weather is important: a fresh wind and some rain and cloud stirs the trout up, especially after long periods of hot weather. Barometric pressure plays an important role, too. Sunshine is bad, and so is thunder.

"My best day illustrates what I'm talking about when it comes to weather. It was about six years ago and the early morning just blew and blew so hard it wasn't fit to go out, not even with my brother. We were cursing, because we don't often get time to

"Sea trout here are seen as a blessed resource, a gift that is not going to be squandered."

DAYS AFLOAT *To bank fish is good, but messing about in boats cannot be bettered. A boat gives you the freedom of the lough. You're free to ride with the drift, to explore the wind channels, and to investigate coves miles from the nearest track.*

ourselves, but you don't take risks on Currane. At about eleven thirty in the morning, the day began to get a little bit better and the gusts died down somewhat. So we decided to go. We began where the river comes into the lake, and I was rowing. My brother fished out his first cast and half way into his second he was playing a salmon. It was like that all the rest of the day – just non-stop action. In the end, we boated five salmon and 11 sea trout, and lost three more salmon and 10 sea trout. It got so that at one stage two flies were proving a hindrance and all we could do was fish just the one on the point. Twenty-nine fish hooked in just five hours – that's quite something when you think how long it takes to land a sea trout. In my mind, they're much better fighters than salmon, and what's in no doubt is that they're much more wary and easily spooked. You can get away with a bad cast over a salmon, but never with a sea trout… it's just off and away.

"This year has been good so far. My best day with a fisherman is one salmon and eight good sea trout. One of my fishermen took six salmon and 38 sea trout in a fortnight, which should be regarded as very good sport indeed for wild fish like these.

"I could never live anywhere else or do anything else. Currane is a lovely lake. It's so pure, yet so close to the sea. Do I begin to take the beauty around here for granted?

GOD'S OWN COASTLINE *It's not possible to have a favourite part of Ireland: it's a country just too rich, too magnanimous, too beautiful for that. But the coastline of Kerry is a hard one to better.*

I live just half a mile from the shore and I'm on the water every waking minute I can be, but it's like every morning is a new day and one I'm looking forward to. I know as I'm getting dressed that I can never predict what's going to happen over the next few hours. You can look at the weather and think about the previous day's sport, but your best assessment will always be a mile off. You can have eight sea trout on the Tuesday and although the Wednesday will be identical, you'll take nothing. This is when the amateurs begin to back off and lose their concentration a bit. If they do get a take, then odds are they will fluff it. I prefer being with those that really concentrate, because I know that if they keep going they will get a chance and we'll have a fish in the boat. Being a guide is not just about knowing the water and the fish – there's a fair bit of people management that goes on as well. You've got to explain to those less experienced that poor days all play their part in the scheme of things. If you can urge them to keep going, then they'll get one in the end, and you've got to make them see that one fish after a hard day is a bigger reward than five fish on an easy one. If you're playing a fish so that your knees are trembling and your head's a-thumping… well, that's what really exciting fishing is all about. Mind you, although we O'Sheas know more than a little about Currane, you're never beyond learning a bit from the

SEA TROUT BAY *The winds and the tides funnel the white trout into the bays, and from there they will ascend the rivers and travel the loughs to their spawning grounds. It is wild fish following their primeval instincts that make Ireland such a sensational place for the angler.*

"You're never beyond learning a bit from the people you take out. The English competition fishers, for instance, have taught us all a lot over here."

THE PROMISE OF SUNRISE *A storm the previous night has blown itself away and the morning dawns quiet, sunlit, and full of promise. It could be that the day will become too hot and the fish will go down deep, but at this moment the anticipation of any true angler begins to buzz like an electric charge.*

people you take out. The English competition fishers, for instance, have taught us all a lot over here. And then there was a Frenchman I went out with a year or so back. He wanted to fish the seashore itself for bass and not the lake. He used his sea-trout rod, but put on a saltwater reel and a floating line, and he used lures about 1½ inches long. It was low water, and we got out there waiting for the approach of the tide. He was fishing amongst all the rocks and the weed in the flow and he was hooking fish after fish – constantly on the move, exploring new water, his rod bent, his reel shrieking. I thought 'I could enjoy some of that.'"

A Changed Man

The next morning, I meet Neil down by his boats. The clouds have lifted and the raging wind has blown itself away. The white horses have ceased their charge and there are shafts of sunlight playing through the broken cloud. It's simply a glorious morning. Neil is much happier, busying himself around the boatshed, putting up rods, checking engines, sorting fly boxes. Anticipation is high: you can feel it tingling in every fibre, and Neil is a changed man from yesterday, when all he could do was talk a good session! Now, he's a man in his element.

Sea Trout Tips

Neil advises a 9ft-6in to 11-ft single-handed rod. This will be allied with either a floating or intermediate line. He's reluctant to let any of his fishermen use leaders less than 6 or 8 pounds in breaking strain. He stresses that trout fresh from the sea will smash 4-lb leaders with ease. Fluorocarbon (Berkley especially) means that you can fish thin and strong at the same time, but you do need to take care of these modern tippet materials. If they become abraded then they can snap unexpectedly and without warning.

- Most flies are tied on hooks between sizes 8 and 14, but Neil will drop to a size 16 in extreme conditions – for example, if the water is low and clear and there's bright sunlight. The basic flies include the Green Peter, the Black Pennell, the Sooty Olive, and Watson's Fancy. The competent angler can wield teams of three flies, but Neil always takes the skill of his angler into account and reduces the number of flies if tangles need to be avoided.

- The flies are fished very close to the surface on a 14- to 15-ft leader with 6-inch droppers for the top two flies. Neil himself would fish 20-ft leaders or even more, but realizes these are difficult to cast, especially from a boat and into a wind.

- He tends to pick drift lanes that take him over the shallow, rocky areas with wildly varying depths. He will pass by islands and over reefs, generally scouting out water less than 30ft deep.

- The best conditions are overcast days with westerly or southerly winds of around 10 to 15 miles an hour, with 20 miles an hour the absolute maximum. The worst conditions are obviously bright sunshine, but even then he'll go out and fish his anglers hard.

WILD WEATHER *You're out there in a force seven, the wind is shrieking, your rods are buckling, and the waves are crashing over the side of your boat. You look at your guide but he's calm and he's concentrating and he knows that a fish is possible before dusk falls. Suddenly, you feel at peace in his hands.*

- It's all daytime fishing on Currane, starting at 9am and finishing at 5 – real office hours! There aren't any particular best periods, and it is vital to concentrate all the time. The fish will simply switch on or off according to their own whim, which makes them impossible to predict. You just have to stay on the case.

- The top of Neil's list of most common mistakes is underestimating the sea trout. These are serious fish that demand an ultra-serious approach. He counts concentration as possibly the greatest gift, and this is why he likes taking out the competition men from the English Midlands. Their focus is hawk-like: they have been brought up in such a hard school that they're virtually professional but, then again, it depends what you want out of the day. You can be highly focused and take half a dozen fish, or be more haphazard and enjoy the holiday, providing you accept that the rewards will inevitably be less.

THE KERRY BLACKWATER
The Perfect Spate River

"I just love these quick, small spate rivers that are up and down like a fiddler's elbow."

As I'm about to leave Waterville, Neil O'Shea tips me off about the Kerry Blackwater, a short spate river just a few miles away emptying into Kenmare River, the bay on the south of the county. I need no urging to have a look: I just love these quick, small spate rivers that are up and down like a fiddler's elbow. Here is the one situation where fishermen are like twitchers and could do with an organization like Birdline!

Quite simply, if you don't hit these rivers exactly right – and I mean exactly – then you've blown it, you're just too late. Fish can come into the swollen river overnight, run and feed wildly the following day, and it can be all over by the second day. Really good small spate river salmon fishermen will drop anything and everything to get to the river when it's at its peak. They know how to make friends with local hotels, ghillies, tackle dealers, anglers, farmers – anyone who has an eye on the water levels. Weather forecasts are watched constantly. The gear is always in the boot of the car. Fishing these small rivers is for the connoisseur: the angler becomes more the hunter, the stalker, on such intimate waters. You need a true feel for water, for you don't fish streams like this with a guide. You are on your own, and it's all down to your personal skill. And, of course, the blessed chance of being there at the right time.

A Lucky Meeting

The track from the main road wandered its attractive way up towards the mountains, and when I pulled in at the anglers' car park, there was a vehicle already there and a familiar-looking face bobbing at the window. Doctor Whelan, I presume! Now, Ken

THE ETERNAL POOL (opposite) *There are times when a fisherman of experience looks at a pool and his heart simply skips. It's just too good, too magnificent not to hold fish. Every crease, every nuance of the current suggests success. Every cast is made not in hope but in expectation.*

SHADOWS IN THE STREAM *Make no mistake about it, spotting fish, fresh-run salmon especially, is a true art form. They come and they go like whispers on the wind. Their very survival depends on anonymity, and you're a heron of a hunter if you can mark them down with regularity.*

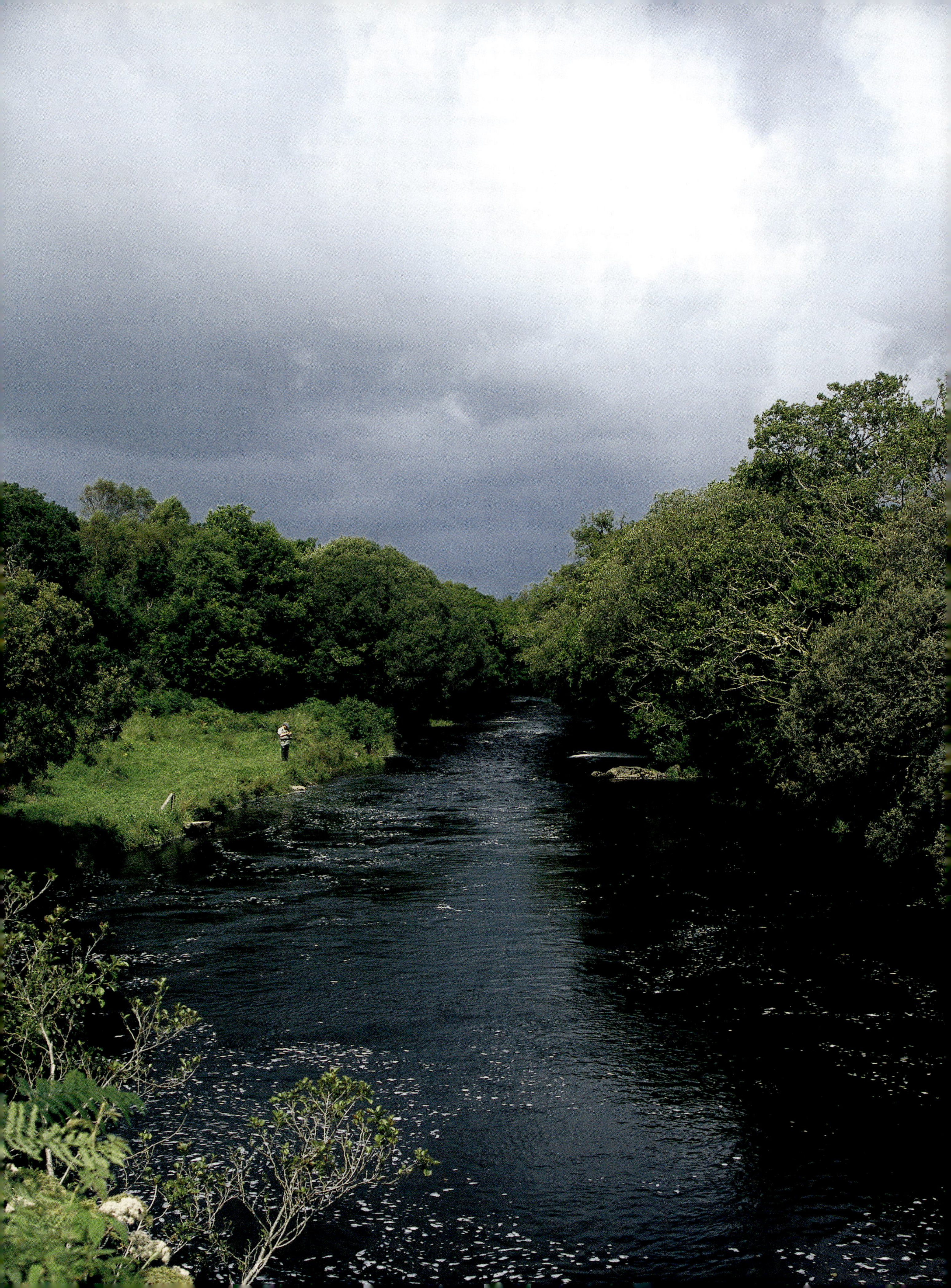

UPON THE POINT OF SUCCESS *You just know it's going to happen. That line now thrumming in the current is suddenly going to twitch and tighten and that blessed moment that all anglers know is only seconds, heartbeats away.*

BESIDE THE STREAM *Sure, your eyes are glued to the water, but look around at the birds, the mating damsel flies, the spiralling mayfly, and the vivid moths as the dusk begins to pull in. Listen to the call of the owl, the cry of the vixen. Angling is the surest route to the heart of the natural world.*

Whelan is one of Ireland's best known, best respected, and most loved fisherman. His book *The Angler in Ireland* has been one of my bibles. His work with the Central Fisheries Board has made him a legend in conservation circles, and it is arguable that no-one in Ireland has had a greater effect on the rejuvenation of fisheries than Ken. Impressive credentials these may be, but they count for nothing beside his warmth, his enthusiasm, his generosity, his intellect, and his bubbling sense of humour. I felt myself extremely fortunate to be standing beside such a wondrous river on such a lovely day in the company of such a man.

"Ireland is full of secrets like this," Ken said. "Go back just a few years and the river wasn't much at all, but it's been taken by the scruff of its neck and really turned round. All credit to James Pembroke, here, for giving us back a little bit of paradise. Ultimately it's all about control, if rivers like this are to flourish. Huge amounts can be done by curbing netting, restricting lice from the fish farms, improving the spawning redds, instituting hatcheries even, but when the river is poached it all comes to nought. You can make sure that poachers will be caught and dealt with, but the real key is education, and that's where James has been so good. He's got the locals to see the river here as a resource. Everyone hereabouts can make good money if tourists are coming in for excellent fishing, and whereas there always used to be tacit support for poachers, it's not the case now. Too much money can be made locally in hotels, guesthouses, bed and breakfasts, restaurants, and shops for a blind eye to be turned to the poacher anymore. Thinking of the airlines, the ferry companies, and the car hire firms, too, we've just got to realize that sport fishing along with golf are the real saviours of the Irish Tourist Board. It certainly can't survive on the weather!

"There's definitely a change in the air. Middle-aged men that once took boot-loads of fish are now keen to fish catch-and-release. Why? For the satisfaction of seeing a fish swim away free, which is immeasurable – and now that legislation makes it impossible for them to sell fish, what's the point of taking more than you can reasonably and quickly eat anyway? Virtually everyone's got the picture now, that it's just gross to haul bagfuls away to the freezer."

I noticed with some delight that Ken was putting a rod up and I sensed that I could be in for a treat. "Of course I don't mind if you tag along, although I don't think you'll learn much from me! To be honest with you, I think we've just missed the best of it. It's the usual thing isn't it? If only we'd been here yesterday. Actually, I was. I got here last evening and walked a mile or two of the river, just soaking it in, thinking how lovely it all was and looking out for fish. I helped a couple of lads land one and we all enjoyed seeing it swim away again. There certainly were plenty of fish in the river just 15 hours ago or so, so we've got a chance, I guess."

Ken's gear was really just heavy trout kit. A 9-ft rod, an 8-weight floating line, a 12-ft, 10-lb breaking strain leader, a sea-trout fly on the dropper, and a small shrimp on the tail to complete the outfit. He would, he said, probably scale down the size of the flies steadily throughout the day.

Fishing with a Master

And off we went, first of all stopping at a deep, slow piece of water that looked dead, dark, and lifeless, the sort of place you usually associate with spinning. "In places like this, you've really got to work the fly, because you can't get the current to do that for you. It'd be my advice to search out the tree line and to cast as far as you can under the branches on the far bank there, because the fish like to hang in the shade. Look really hard for your fish, because you'll sometimes see them hanging in mid-water, and keep your nerve when they come after the fly. Don't strike or pull it out in your excitement. Wait for them to catch it, turn, and move the line before you lift into them. Water like this is frequently overlooked and it shouldn't be, because a lot of fish like to rest up out of the white water."

From there we moved down onto a perfect pool. The flow was channelled between the far bank and a rock outcrop on our side that served as a very tasty fishing platform. A line of alders and oaks hung over the main current, and Ken flicked his flies downstream under the branches. He fished the killing point with devilish intensity as the flies swung round in the current and hung there for an instant. We both sensed the moment when a take was most likely so strongly that, believe me,

A WORLD OF HIS OWN *The rest of the world doesn't exist for Ken. Work, worries, family, bills... nothing exists for him but his line, his fly, and the patch of water that he's working with demonic concentration. "What do you think about when you're fishing?" A true angler just laughs at such a question.*

breathing was difficult. The sun was out, glinting off the dancing water, piercing the tree canopy with darts of light. Squadrons of damselflies crisscrossed the river. A perfect day.

We soon came upon a very quick little run, really nothing more than a thimbleful of water bubbling between two rapids. It was the size of a small sitting room, about three feet deep and quite, quite probably a holding pool for three or four fish. Ken decided on a single fly on the point for such a tiny little pot, coloured orange to suit the still peat-stained water. And then he fished it beautifully. You'd have to say he was flicking the line out rather than casting it, just bouncing the flies down with the flow and twitching them back, searching intently. The retrieve was all done with a neat figure-of-eight action – it's not good to have a lot of loose line out in a situation like this in case a hooked fish manages to make the downstream rapid and you've got to follow at a canter. I noticed, too, that he put a lot of rod top work into the retrieve, constantly jiggling the fly into life. He mended the line continuously, keeping in direct contact throughout the entire cast and then, right at the end of the retrieve, he held the rod high and skated the fly hither and thither in the current. You just never know when an intrigued salmon might be following to your feet.

Ken gave every one of these small pools about 15 minutes of very hard, concentrated fishing. Every nook was searched: these small river fish aren't big, and they can literally melt into the tiniest pocket of water. You've got two chances: a new fish could enter the pool and be instantly vulnerable, or a resident fish could finally be needled into making a mistake, so whilst it's tempting to keep on the move, don't sacrifice thoroughness on each and every pool.

"We soon came upon a very quick little run, really nothing more than a thimbleful of water bubbling between two rapids."

WATCHING FOR ILLUSIONS *Bottom contours are everything to migrating fish. They are their road signs, their railway platforms, their entire means for travel upstream. Look for rocks and fallen branches and there you will find fish. When running salmon are on the move, their progress can be lightning quick, especially in low, clear water when they feel insecure and are searching out deeper, more shaded spots. In fact, you're looking for illusions – hints and shadows – rather than the fish themselves.*

On the next pool downstream, an alder craned helpfully over the river and I climbed it to watch. That orange fly certainly had a life of its own, flicking across the current like a small anguished fish looking for sanctuary. And as my eyes grew accustomed to the water, I sensed the presence of salmon. Two of them. One was around six pounds and almost certainly not a taker. Its head was down and its body language was all dullness and sulkiness. The fly passed just a foot or so away from its head but its fins didn't even flicker. You might just as well have been fishing to a log. The other fish, however, seemed for several minutes to be in half a mind to take. There's no doubt it could see the fly, for whenever it got to within two or even three feet the head would come up and the body angled provocatively. The fins would work and you could almost sense the muscles flex. On one occasion the fish even moved forward in a short burst towards the fly, before easing off and dropping down in the water. There was obviously a third fish in the pool, too, because Ken soon had a strong, solid pull on the far side of the run where the tree shadow divided the water into light and dark. He was unlucky to miss it. Damn.

MOVING ON DOWNSTREAM

Anyway, to another pool, slightly larger this time. "There just has to be one at the tail there." We looked and just knew it had to be so. Ken waded more deeply, fishing the tightest possible line, determined not to miss another take. In reality, he was just dibbling the fly back over where salmon had to be lying. "I'll be flabbergasted if there's no… and the water's just perfect… " Ken was a magician of action and movement, making his fly seemingly impossible to resist. But nothing.

At last we reached the end of the stretch and found a proper pool by normal salmon fishing standards. It lay around 80 yards long, and Ken dibbled his flies over the neck and then worked the main body of the water, moving fast. He cast at 40 degrees or so downstream, the flies all but kissing the far bank, and then pulled them slowly, a foot at a time, across the flow. There was nothing mechanical about this. He varied the retrieve rate and action constantly. Watching his hands was a revelation: sometimes fast, sometimes slow. A pause. A twitch. A jab, and then a long, steady heave. He worked quickly: a cast and then a good pace downriver. The process was repeated again and again with cautious, heron-like concentration. It was a lovely pool – all moving water with no big slacks or back eddies, and not too deep. Once again, from the high bank, I could see salmon here and there whenever the sun broke through the cloud and glinted off their bodies.

He was done. Fishing like this is absolutely exhausting, because you're not only working hard physically but your mind is riveted to the job. To stand a chance of tricking these wary fish, your concentration has to be total. He decided on a couple of hours' break and then he'd fish the dusk, when salmon are always more active, stimulated by the coming night. We walked back upriver towards the fishermen's hut.

WALKING WITH WATER *If there is one thing better than either fishing from the bank or from a boat, it's wading. You feel the thrust of the river against your legs. You know when you're close to the fish. You feel at one with the world of water, no longer alien but embraced by the stream that you love.*

QUINTESSENTIAL IRELAND *Where else in Europe could this photograph conceivably have been taken? There's something about an Irish river valley, so calm, so green, so utterly alluring to anyone with an ounce of fisherman in his body. Don't neglect the deep, tree-lined water above rapids. Fish love to hang there, especially in the brightness of the day.*

THE ROLE OF GOVERNMENT

"The state has to play its part too," he said. "The government has shown it can tackle commercial netting and fish farming to a greater or lesser degree. Rod fishermen who don't like voluntary rules should be made to fish under mandatory ones. Governments have to realize it is impossible to placate everyone at election times, and the greater good must be striven for.

"I'm pleased that the state buys fisheries that have fallen into disrepair, just as it did this one, well over a decade ago. They can then get men of experience to build them up, but then why not transfer them to private ownership and let the river restorers get on with the next project? The old argument goes that this would be unfair to locals because prices would go up. I'm not sure about this, because my guess is that all visitors would, or certainly should, accept a two-tier price system."

I have to agree. After all, every angler coming to Ireland should really take on board that they're guests in a fabulously welcoming country. A proper payment for licence, boat, and guide goes with this privilege. But it's not the same for the local angler: he should, by rights, pay a lesser fee for, after all, he is the ears and eyes of the river, guarding against poaching and pollution. It's he (or she) who must bear the brunt of the new ways and the new rules. It's also the local angler who will be attending the meeting in the winter, when the guests are gone and the summer is no more than a golden memory or a cherished snapshot. It's the local out there in the cold of winter on the working party, clearing overgrown spawning streams or restoring the bankside. In short, there's ample room for visitors and locals alike, providing the fisheries are maintained and the fish continue to thrive there. You could say the future's good here. I'd say the future of fishing is emerald green!

DANCING WATER *It's the water that really dances and sings and pulls and tugs at your line that makes your heart leap. It's here that you know fish are lying, alert in the current, their fins on the twitch, bodies poised for action. Every second of every cast is spent with bated breath. There's never a moment when the line might not conceivably zip tight.*

BUNDORRAGHA RIVER
Restoring the Delphi Fishery

"Delphi is unchanging. This setting amidst mountain, lough, and river is unparalleled."

Joseph Adams made a good stab at describing the beauty that is Delphi, a place that's captivated all who have ever fished it, when he wrote, "From a scenic point of view, Delphi is a perfect gem in a mountain setting. When the sun strikes its oft-times unruffled water, the jewel flashes. Mysterious lights play amongst the facets, and shadows in deep recesses add contrasting charms. Often, far up in the hilltops, a storm is brewed that sweeps down the valley on impetuous feet, lashing the water into foaming anger and turning a peaceful scene into a thing possessed."

"Everyone has heard of Delphi," wrote Walter Peard in his account of a fishing tour of Ireland, *A Year of Liberty*, published some 130 years ago. To him, Delphi was simply "Elysium piscatorium". Nothing has changed. I first saw Delphi 20 years ago and gasped. This year, I gasp again. Delphi is unchanging. This setting amidst mountain, lough, and river is unparalleled. Little wonder that a particular Marquis of Sligo should compare this special place with the wonders of Italy and Greece. However, if beauty can be skin deep on a human visage, so it seems can it be on a landscape, so whilst you can, and should, fall instantly in love with Delphi, it's important to realize that momentous developments have tortured her soul.

This is an old scandal that just won't go away. You've read about it in the context of Inagh and Ballynahinch, and it's an affliction affecting most of Connemara. It's the sad story of the sea trout. You don't need to go back to the days of Adams or Peard to find that Delphi was once a supreme sea-trout water. Even 20 years ago, Delphi was a vibrant sea-trout system, and salmon were an occasional summer bonus.

TIMELESS DELPHI (opposite) *The top of the Delphi system is shrouded in mist, magic, and history. This is a place that has seen the despair of famine and the elation of generations of anglers. It's lonesome and lovely, and it is views like this that take you to the core of what the sport is all about.*

A WORLD OF WATER *There can be few countries with more inland water than Ireland. In fact, after many hundreds of miles driving from coast to coast, I almost defy you to show me any route of more than ten miles that doesn't cross or accompany a river, a lake, or an upland tarn. And all this water is beautiful – waterfalls, hidden valleys, pools reflecting misty mountains.*

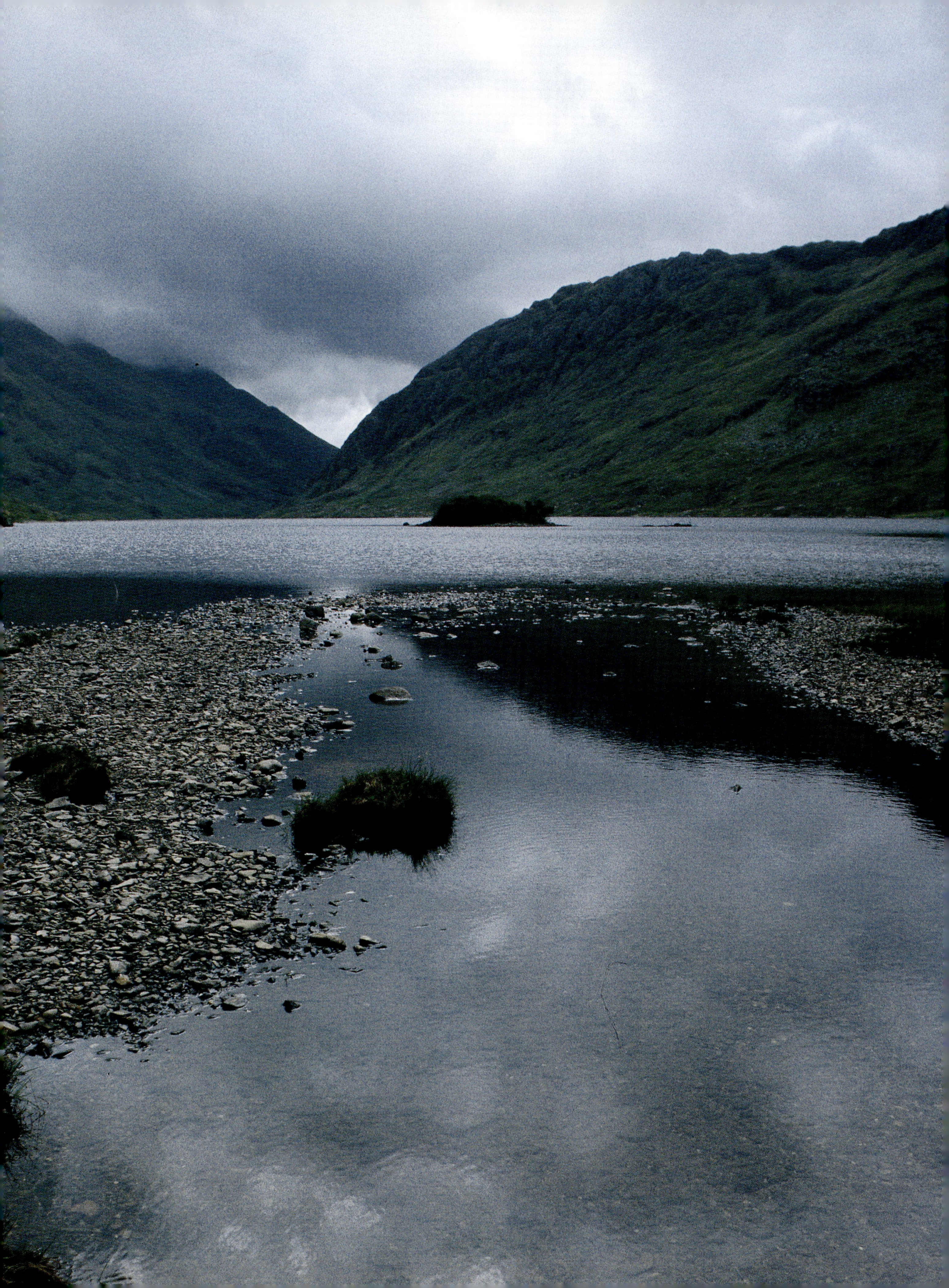

THE HATCHERY *The modern Delphi has made its name through the most advanced of fishery management techniques. It's a tribute to the fishery that it combines the artificial with the natural, the manufactured with the wild. Here is a fishery that shows a sensitivity from which all can learn.*

Catastrophe and Drastic Measures

Then the fish farms came to Killary Harbour at the mouth of the Bundorragha River, the gateway to the Delphi fishery – and the sea-trout stocks collapsed. As Peter Mantle, the present owner of Delphi, says, "Through 1988 and 1989 we experienced what can only be called a sea-trout catastrophe. Delphi's whole reputation and clientèle was based on sea-trout fishing, and suddenly the flow was reduced to a trickle. We were like a pub with no beer. We had the choice of packing up or doing something about it. We'd always had an interesting run of salmon, but that had been incidental – probably about 100 fish a year and merely a bonus. Now we realized we must either develop the salmon fishing or go under. The science of the decision was quite secondary: everything we did was out of simple, economic necessity. We gambled everything – back then a huge 130,000 Euros – in trying to engineer, at the very least, a larger grilse run. And the gamble paid off.

"We opened the hatchery in 1990, released smolts in the spring of 1991, and had our first returns during the summer of 1992. To our amazement, and that of the scientists, the fish we released, which were of three different origins, all performed very differently. Firstly, there was the Delphi brood stock itself, then ranched fish from Burrishoole, near Newport in County Mayo, and the third source was the government hatchery itself at Cong, so they were, therefore, Corrib fish. What happened is fascinating. It soon appeared that the Burrishoole fish performed very strongly as grilse, which looked after our late spring and summer fishing. Our own Delphi fish didn't perform as grilse, but excelled as early running, large springers. The Corrib fish performed in a mediocre fashion and we dropped them. The net result is that we now have a big spring run and a large grilse run, and we've managed to maintain a good proportion of fish derived from the wild Delphi stock itself."

DILIGENT MANAGEMENT

Naturally, the Delphi hatchery was expensive to inaugurate – it still costs more than 100,000 Euros each year to run, but it's not just the expense that raises questions. There are a huge number of complex moral and biological issues as well, and Peter is quite open about the ambiguity. In an ideal world, it would never occur to him to run the hatchery, but in a flawed one, what are the choices? Remove Delphi Lodge and the Delphi fishery from the Connemara angling scene, and the local economy really does stare into a black hole. Every shred of opinion I've picked up on in Ireland has been on Peter's side over this, especially when you consider how carefully he is running the whole hatchery operation.

"We are constantly afraid of compromising the genetic purity of the wild Delphi fish, and we do everything in our power to lessen the impact of the hatchery. For example, throughout January we anaesthetize, fin-clip, and tag 50,000 salmon pre-smolts, so that we can identify them at a later date as hatchery fish rather than wild ones. It's a horrid, cold job, but it's essential. Then follows a huge after-season netting programme to take out hatchery fish before they can get to the redds and interfere with Delphi salmon there. We use the eggs from these fish for our own hatchery and we also send them to ambitious projects on the Rhine and the Thames.

"Our hatchery has attracted attention, and it is hugely expensive and difficult to justify financially, but it's something we have to do if we're to remain. There's obviously controversy attached to it, and I would never recommend a hatchery just for the sake of it, but what do you do in the face of a totally ruined sea-trout fishery? Nor would I hold up anything I've done as a model. We have managed to keep Delphi as a healthy system, still producing the same number of wild smolts as before. It's just that the wild ones on their own aren't enough to provide sport, and it's on sport that the whole business depends. It looks as though things are working here, but I warn anybody against messing with wild fisheries just for the sake of it. There are certain places, like the Ranga River in Iceland, where there are no fish at all to begin with, and where hatcheries can prove invaluable. At least now at Delphi we are on the map as a salmon fishery, and we have reinvented ourselves. Because of the hatchery, we've increased salmon catches by up to 500 percent, and the spring salmon mean we can now operate all year round, which is vital for the area's employment."

"There's obviously controversy attached to it, and I would never recommend a hatchery just for the sake of it..."

MUSIC TO YOUR EARS *Waterfalls are magical places that simply sing out to the angler and drown out any alien sound. Fish near a waterfall and you do become part of another world in a way that's hard for a non-angler to understand.*

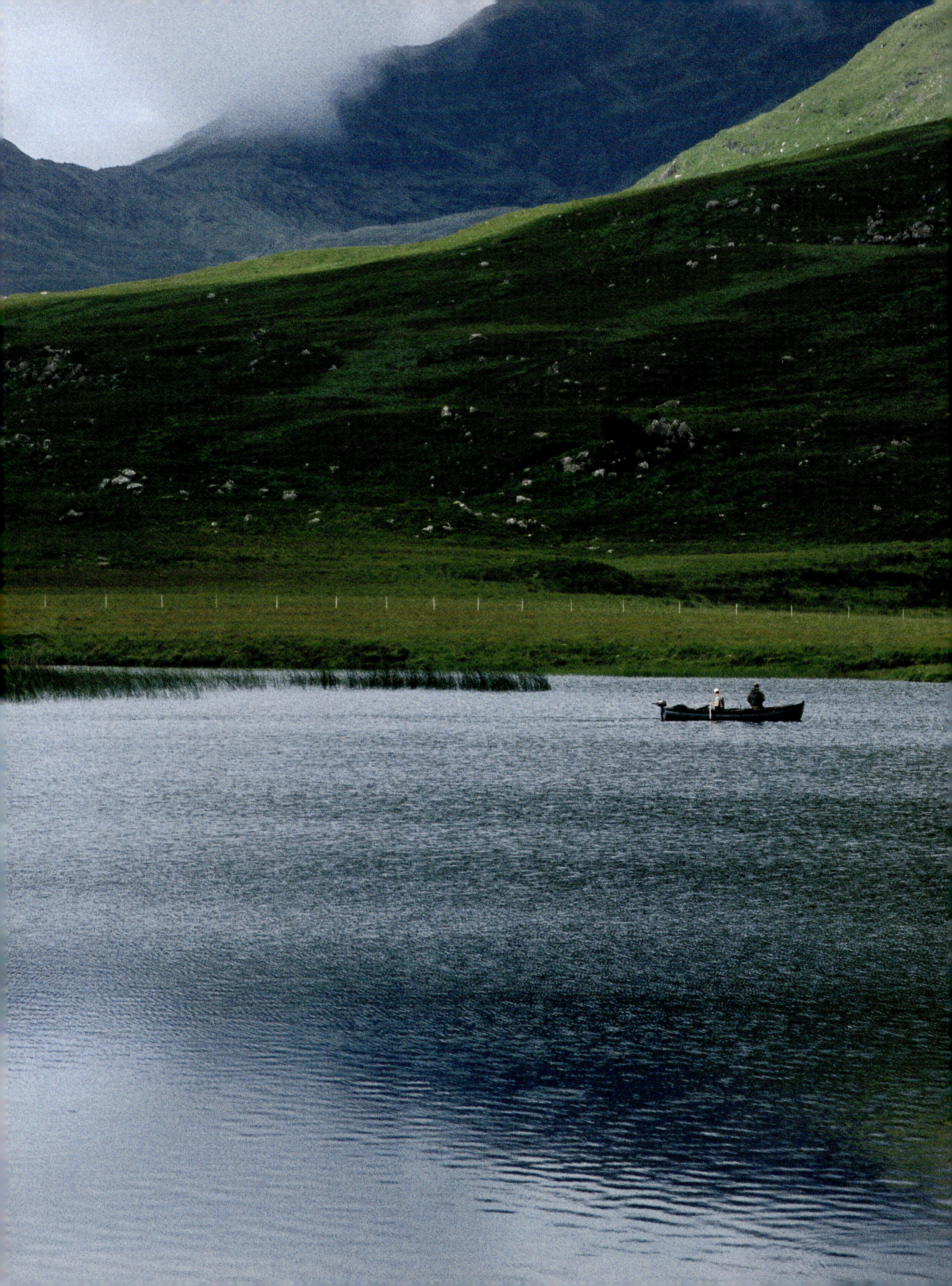

Natural Differences

It is, of course, the differing behavioural patterns of sea trout smolts and salmon smolts that have allowed Delphi to live on as a vibrant fishery. Peter only releases smolts into the system, not fry or par. These go straight to sea, so they don't interfere with the freshwater phase of the wild fish at all. In fact, Delphi-tagged fish have been found off the Faro Islands after just a few weeks. The natural Delphi smolts travel up to the west coast of Greenland, from where tags have been sent back by Inuit fisheries. These fish don't come back until they've spent two winters at sea. They then hit the Bundorragha River between January and May as big springers, and Delphi opens the season for them from February onwards.

Sea trout smolts, however, operate quite differently, tending to be much more coastal and estuarine dwelling. In fact, they often won't leave their home river mouth by any great distance at all, and herein lies the crux of the problem – the amount of sea lice generated by many fish farms. In Killary Harbour, site of the farm, there is little exchange of water. The tide mooches in and out and the lice are not swept away. Instead, they form a huge, debilitating soup that chokes the lifeblood out of the sea trout populations in the area. The salmon can run through it on their way out and on their way back: they don't have to try to live with it like the sea trout.

Of course, there are better and worse fish farms. If sites are sensitively placed, with water moving through the cages at all times, the offending lice will be carried away and scattered through the ocean. Fish farms in sea loughs may be safe from gales and easy to manage, but they are environmentally hugely dangerous. The density of fish in the cages is also of paramount importance. All salmon have diseases endemic within them, but the more they are crowded and the greater the stress they live their lives under, the more their immune response is compromised. If a fish farm is badly or greedily run, the chances of salmon expressing diseases is greatly enhanced. To farm fish well, therefore, requires low cage densities and proper siting.

The Enduring Allure of Delphi

So what of "Elysium piscatorium"? Our sad commercial age seems to take us a universe away from such a concept, but it shouldn't do. Delphi Lodge remains a simply magnificent place to visit and to fish, combining all the best elements from all the best fishing lodges around the world. During my brief stay, the staff were lively, fun, and informative, and the guests were having a ball. Casting tuition was being given on the lawns of the house, salmon were leaping in the loughs, and anglers were stalking up and down the river. When we assembled for lunch, everyone was full of stories. Sandwiches and soup were wolfed down, as anticipation for the afternoon grew, and I found myself sipping my coffee amidst a clatter of pushed-back chairs. Dinner proved to be a more relaxed occasion, but I guess many woke up impatiently throughout the night to urge on the slow-moving hands of their alarm clocks!

ON THE DRIFT (opposite) *Delphi doesn't just offer superb river fishing – the lakes, too, can be absolutely crammed with in-coming salmon. The sight of a late summer fish rising to a cranefly imitation is one of the most exciting I have ever witnessed.*

DON'T SPOOK THE FISH WITH TESTOSTERONE

Although Ireland offers less pressured fishing than anywhere else in Europe, you can still mess up by being unguarded and spooking wild fish, and I have to say that women seem far less prone to some of the mistakes that men tend to make.

CARE AT THE WATER SIDE

Let's start with your approach. It's dawn, and you're at the riverbank. Look hard in the dew or, if you're after pike in the winter, the frost. Are there footprints? If there are, tread resolutely in the opposite direction. You're not being anti-social, but the probability is that if you're not the first, someone else has blown your chances clean away.

Whatever you do, remember that sound is intensified by roughly a factor of five under water. This is massive, so, if you can, choose the grass or a mud bank rather than gravel. Above all, watch those footsteps. Women have the advantage here of smaller feet and lighter weight but, above all, they don't show that same self-defeating urge to hurry to the waterside, so the rumble factor underwater is slashed in their favour.

The same thing goes for women's voices, which are generally softer. If you're a man, try listening to your own excited, bragging tones and those of your braying friends. Keep it down. Talk in quiet tones or not at all.

The colour and texture of your clothing are also important. Think drab. Think soft. A hat's good, if only to shield the flash thrown when the sun strikes your pale face. And think about that tackle vest or heavy bag. Do you need all the clattering, glittering gizmos? Women seem to be less fixated on gadgets, less encumbered, and they move more quietly as a result.

You obviously walk upriver, simply because you're approaching fish from behind, but think how you walk. Be aware of your shadow. Be especially conscious that the shadow lengthens as the sun sinks. Even a quickly raised pointing finger can spook the fish. It's particularly important to avoid scaring small fish at the margins, because they flee and trigger off a chain reaction of fear throughout the water. If the water is clear and shallow, it's best to creep and crawl and make yourself as unobtrusive as a mouse.

A LIFE TO COME *Release all parr and baby browns carefully, without taking them out of the water and without touching their delicate, glorious little bodies. Remember that their life is still to come, and it will be one full of danger and challenge.*

Above all, make that first cast count. Don't be impetuous, in the way most males are. If you've got a guide, listen to him. Watch the lie and take your time until you've worked out a strategy. The more casts you put over any piece of water, the further your chances fall, so quell the hormones, slow your beating heart, and try to reveal a patience that isn't naturally yours.

ANTI-SPOOKING SKILLS

If you're not to scare the fish off on a regular basis then, besides taking care in the ways I've outlined, there are certain skills that you really should learn.

Fish can see you, so learn to see them first, so that you can pick them out and plot their undoing. Obviously, you need polarizing glasses (although a horrifying percentage of anglers fail to use them). Binoculars, too, can be hugely useful, even close up, for identifying fish and what they are feeding upon.

On thin, clear water you must learn to cast a long leader if you're to avoid lining a fish. Put a fly line over a wild trout or grayling and it's goodbye. It's the same when bait fishing. This is why "holding back" a float is so important when trotting for grayling or roach: the first thing the fish sees is the bait and not the shot, which, as often as not, raps it on the nose.

Learn to cast lying down on your back, or at a crouch, or on your stomach. Learn to roll cast and spiral cast so that trees are no problem. Cast slowly and methodically, not jerkily, and think about your silhouette all the time. You only have to strive for distance when you've spooked the fish, and by striving you spook them more and more. Don't become the human windmill. Don't false cast more than you have to. If you can put out the line required in a single cast, do it.

Try to cast a foot above the water so that your line and fly fall lightly. "Feather" your spool if you're bait or lure fishing. Remember that accuracy is more important than distance.

Don't be a slave to your tackle. Buy the best, maintain it in top condition, and don't concern yourself about it again. This is important when it comes to fly lines. Buy high quality and keep them clean, and they will zing out with minimum casting effort and less destructive arm action above the water line. Dull down your leader – rub it in the dirt if necessary.

Don't rush in when you're spinning or fly fishing on a still water. Put a couple of casts down each margin before exploring the water in front of you, or you'll scare any close-in fish – try to catch it first.

Use any natural disturbance to help mask your own unnatural intrusion upon the fish. For instance, fish close to a feeding swan – but not so close that you run the risk of hooking it. If you see drinking cattle, get close to them and flick a fly immediately downstream. You might even kick up a little silt yourself, to colour the water. Use any floating weed to break up the silhouette of your fly line. If you're trout fishing in crystal water, then a strike indicator could alarm a really wily shoal. Take it off and tie on a piece of twig or a sliver of reed.

Take on board what I've said, and you'll find your chances and your pleasures increase. You're welcome to ignore it all if you choose, and remain the clod who sends the fish fleeing in panic everywhere he goes. Blame your failures on anything but yourself. There'll just be more fish for the rest of us.

SCOUTING MISSION *Don't rush into any fishing situation, especially on a small, clear river like this one. Take time to assess the contours of the pool and where the fish are lying. Spend a day walking and considering and you'll find a whole week is made more successful.*

THE WESTERN LOUGHS
Corrib and Mask in Summer

"You don't even have to know that the wild brown trout fishing here is probably the best in Europe to be entranced."

Water is beautiful, and it doesn't matter where you view Corrib or Mask from, providing there is sunlight, your soul will melt. These are sceptred lakes set in a wonderful, rural landscape. You don't even have to know that the wild brown trout fishing here is probably the best in Europe to be entranced.

As the summer wore on, I set about meeting up with two more lough maestros – Basil Shiels and Roy Peirce. It's so common to find Irish guides who are living branches of a ghillying family tree that it's refreshing to find in Basil what you might term a self-made man. Yes, of course Basil had always fished, although his early years were spent more on loughs Erne and Melvin, and he'd only ever tackled Corrib on and off before 1989. It was also his misfortune to arrive in Galway at the start of the Irish boat strike, which, of course, virtually halted fishing for two hard years. Basil has certainly made up for that since, and it's fascinating to hear how he has transformed himself into one of the top guides on the lough today. Between 1992 and 1994, Basil fished the lough as hard as he possibly could, but the going was tough. He couldn't really form an overall picture of what the water was saying to him. So, in 1995, he sold his business and dedicated himself to Corrib. That season he spent every single day out on the lough – yes, 228 consecutive days with a fly rod in his hand. He mentally and spiritually immersed himself in the lough, opening himself to its every message, to every hint that it gave him. Basil is now rightly regarded as one of the masters of the water.

Basil is not only revered for his knowledge, but also for his bubbling enthusiasm. Listening to him talk, you have to remind yourself that he's a grown man, not a

SPARKLING WATER (opposite) *Lough Corrib is a jewel of a water. Not only are its brown trout stocks to be marvelled at, but its setting, too, is quite magical. This truly is a lake you could spend a lifetime on and never grow tired of fishing.*

MAN AT PEACE *Roy Peirce afloat on Lough Corrib. It's a cliché, I know, but he really does know this vast inland water like the back of his hand. This knowledge has brought so much pleasure to so many anglers throughout the years.*

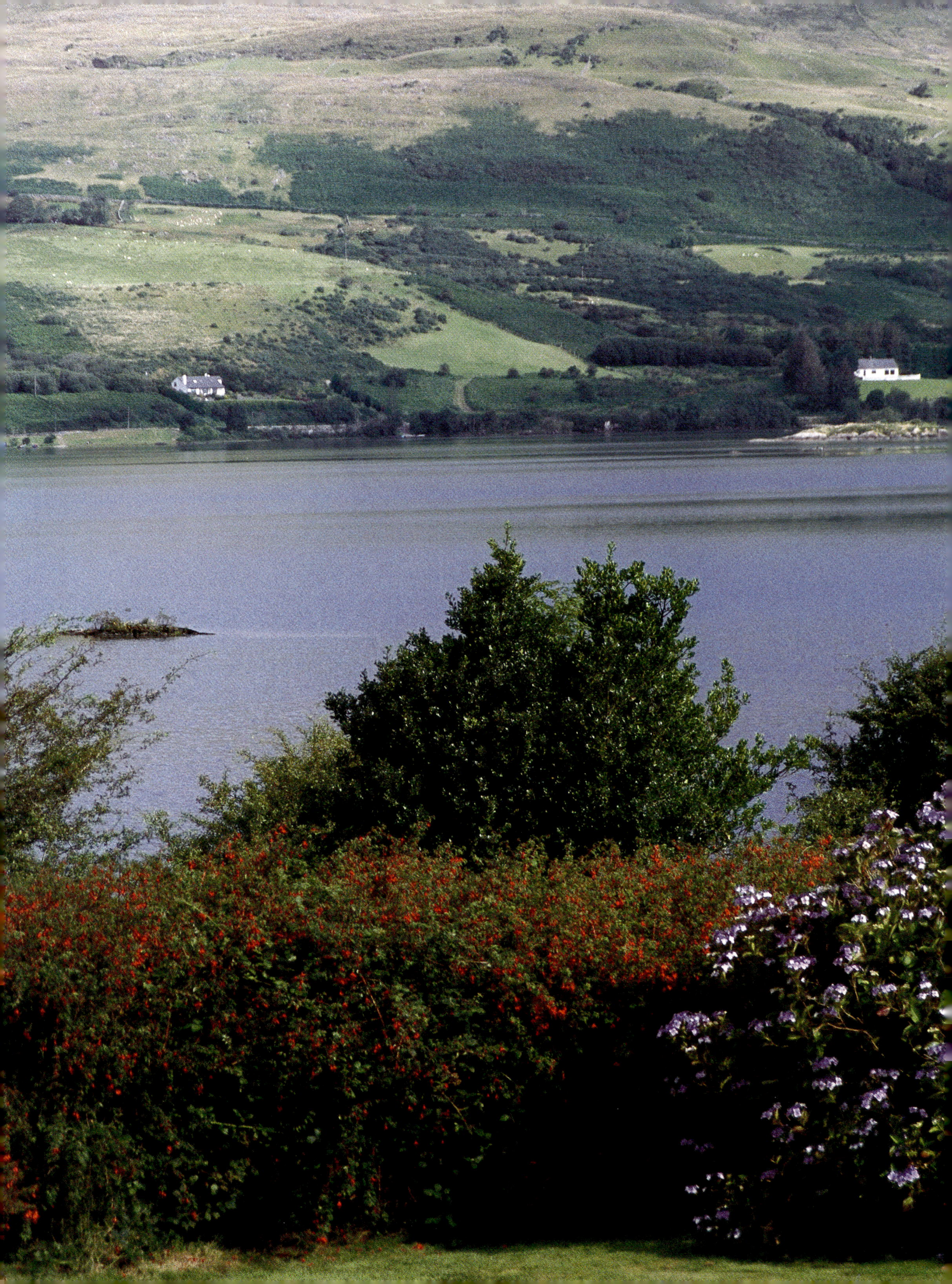

AS THE SUN SETS *Corrib takes on its most mysterious and awesome mood as the sun starts to sink and the shadows spread across it. Soon the wind will die down, insects will begin to hatch, and you can expect the trout to feed until the early hours of the morning.*

gushing teenager in the throes of his first love – for love is certainly what Basil feels for Corrib. It shows when you're on the water with him. He's got a story about every spit, every point, island, and rocky outcrop. You feel he knows each and every trout by name, and he fishes for them with a demonic energy and concentration. This would be off-putting were it not for the fact that you can see he's having tremendous, knockout fun. Basil is a busy fisherman, because he's not out there to waste time. His knowledge is encyclopaedic, but he's still learning, and he knows he always will be, and that's what keeps every single day out with his clients so fresh and exciting.

Every aspect of Corrib fishing excites him. "At the start of the season you'll find the trout in Corrib going mad for brickeen, the minnows. Minkies are the artificial equivalent, and fishing with them can be genuinely thrilling. The duck fly is great, but so are the olives and the mayfly. Sedge fishing is fun, and so is hunting trout hooked on daphnia. The key to fishing any of the styles lies in the confidence of knowing the water and following your hunch based on years of experience."

GRASSHOPPER COTTAGE

There are few fishermen who wouldn't swap lives with Roy Peirce. His lodge stands on the spectacular Dooras Peninsula, and Corrib lies no more than a decent cast from his sitting room. Roy, like Basil, has a knowledge of the lough to make you gasp, but he, too, is still learning, often from his own visitors. "Foreign anglers have revolutionized fishing on the lough. It used to be much more haphazard, and if conditions weren't right, then you simply didn't bother going out. You certainly wouldn't have even known about the vast range of techniques that can winkle out fish in any conditions today. Before buzzers, different sink rate lines, new leader materials, and the influence of the Chew and Grafham men, I guess this was just a sleepy backwater. Guests and ideas come from all over. We had this Russian chap, and all he wanted to do was walk down to the bottom of the garden and fish small shrimp patterns from the bank into the bay. Now, the lake is full of shrimps, but I'd never really considered them much until our Russian friend came along. He did nothing else for the week, but he amassed huge numbers of trout, perch, and roach, too.

"In recent years, we've made great strides here in catching the daphnia feeders, and that's really opened up our summer sport. You're here now in August and it's flat, calm, and bright, and although we'd probably struggle out there, we would catch daphnia feeders providing we could locate them. They're often over very deep water, 100 feet plus, but you'll catch them right on the top if conditions are right. On hot, bright days the daphnia go deep, pulling the trout down with them, but when it's dull the daphnia banks stay up and the catches can be incredible. Two years ago, for example, I had a fantastic day rising 80 fish and landing 25 of them. Remember that Corrib is a really searching lough, and after 40 years on it I can tell you that four fish for a day is very good going indeed. Imagine what we made of 25!

"If you are here in the high summer and you want to search for the daphnia feeders, then you've really got to invest in a good boatman. Remember that the banks of daphnia aren't enormous. They might be 200 yards long, perhaps, but only 30 or so yards wide, and they're scattered over huge areas of water. A boatman should have learnt the likely spots – from experience, from watching other anglers, and from talking to his colleagues. Boatmen can cross-reference points on the lough that would baffle anyone without their experience. The duck fly and mayfly fishing is comparatively simple because, of course, you see the fish breaking the surface, but with daphnia feeders it's quite different, and water depth becomes a major factor.

"I'm always trying new tippet materials, and it pays off when you're searching for daphnia feeders. Fluorocarbons have helped enormously, and you can now fish six-pound breaking strain tippets without any fear of breaking off on a big fish. I like to fish long, fine, and fast with flies that have a bit of flash in them. Look at my fly desk – all greens and golds, just perfect for high summer. The red-arsed Green Peter, the Soldier Palmers, the Octopus, the Raymond – all great flies."

"In recent years, we've made great strides here in catching the daphnia feeders, and that's really opened up our summer sport."

SPOTTED WONDER *There's just something about Corrib brown trout that puts them amongst the favourite of game fish anywhere in the world. Perhaps it's the spotting patterns, or their fullness of shape and the perfection of their fins. Perhaps it's the rich, deep, ingrained colouring, or the fact that they fight like leopards. No doubt it's all these things, as well as their glorious setting.*

GRILSE, FEROX, AND BROWN TROUT

"I'd say to any anglers coming out here in July that a day or two targeting the grilse in the lough is a really viable and exciting proposition. You can catch them on dry flies, and the anticipation level in the boat can be sky high. Ideally, you need a stormy day – one perhaps just a notch below being unfishable. You can drift almost endlessly, skittering mayfly patterns as you go. On one single July drift, I once rose 12 grilse. Mind you, I didn't actually land any, but the excitement... well you can guess! The grilse fishing is good, but I reckon if the drift nets were lifted at sea it would become a really viable proposition, a product we could properly market.

"There are, obviously, huge ferox trout on Corrib if you like trolling. They've almost certainly benefited from the roach explosion, which in its turn has pretty well annihilated the char population. The size of the ferox can distort the true facts of the fishery. In 30 or 40 years of fishing the Corrib, I've only had three trout over five pounds on the fly. I've known many people fish Corrib all their lives and never have a fly-caught five-pounder. No, it's the wild browns of between one-and-three-quarter and two-and-a-quarter pounds that are the pure gold for us, the fish that keep drawing anglers back year upon year. It's these fish that are our bread and butter. The lake holds huge quantities of them, and it could be that catch-and-release has helped in this respect. Where once everything was taken away, I guess now at least 85 percent go back. It's also interesting that on the Corrib there are even regional differences amongst the fish stocks. For example, you'll catch a torpedo-shaped trout, which is an open lake fish. Some trout have rounded tail fins that are a bit flabby, and these are weed-bed fish that don't move much and just gorge on insects. Then you've got noticeably sharp-tailed trout, and these are deep-water fish, often daphnia feeding. The spotting patterns change as you move around the lake, and very frequently you'll find subtle changes in belly colour that reflect the ground they've been feeding over."

Roy's wife, Sorcha, brings us the most delectable fresh scones that I've ever tasted. The lodge is being cleaned for the next influx of anglers and the air has that sweet tang about it of a freshly scrubbed house. "All the guests want different things. Some of them fish intensely, but many are just here for the atmosphere, the craick, the landscape, and nights in the village pub. Fishing is fun and a fish is a bonus. All types keep coming back and back over the years, but I'll admit that I've got particular affection for a group that call themselves the Roy's Mushroom Pickers' Club! It's almost impossible to get them off the mushroom meadows and onto the water."

THE FISHING MATCH

Roy has tipped me off about a big fishing match being held on Mask and its sister lough, Carra. If ever there will be an opportunity to see what these waters can yield up, this is going to be it. And now it's 6.50pm and I'm standing in the car park of a pub a couple of miles outside the town of Ballinrobe. The sun is setting, and the daylong shadows are lengthening around the strange gallows creation set up to receive the competitors' trout. On a stage close by, the scales glisten with judicial splendour. The cups are freshly buffed and shining. The array of shields would do justice to a Roman battalion. The prizes are laid out, and if you're a skilled fly fisherman hereabouts, you obviously won't go short of anything from a vacuum cleaner to a freshly prepared pig.

A barbecue is lit and the smell is tantalizing. The scales men pace around, glancing at their watches, looking this way and that, up and down the road. The pub's doors and windows are flung open, and the siren scent of beer drifts on the balmy late summer evening's air. The children are playing, and the atmosphere buzzes. But where are the fishers? This is like a wedding without the bride. The scales men, the spectators, and I all squint into the falling sun. Again and again, we all look up the road towards Carra and then down the road at Mask. It's 6.55. A dribble of cars swings into view. 6.56. A flood. 6.58. An avalanche. 6.59. The last desperate few hammer into the car park, tyres squealing. Seven o'clock and that's your lot!

It has been a hard day: bright sun is bad, but bright sun and a breeze combined is far worse. And it's August, too, traditionally a tricky month even if the weather is with you. But there are fine fish to see and the star of them all is a truly splendid speckled four-and-a-half-pound brown, taken as the light began to slant away.

Several hundred trout hang from their gibbets, and what Roy told me is absolutely true: the anglers can identify the origin of virtually every fish. The 4½-pounder, with its golden stomach, is from a deep sandy bay. The smaller, heavily speckled fish are from Carra. I must try Carra, I'm told – its water a green turquoise blue that makes you think you're fishing the tropics. It's so clear, though, that you can often see the fish take, something that never happens on Corrib or Mask. For an Irish angler to get excited, Carra really must be some experience!

END OF THE DAY *So this is it. The match is over and the fish have been brought back to be weighed. A sad sight? Well, the fish certainly won't be wasted. They'll be cleaned, cooked, and served up with vegetables in kitchens all around the area.*

TOTAL FLY FISHING
Casting for Alternatives

"... there isn't a fish that swims that won't take a fly of one design or another..."

I've hinted at this once or twice before: if the water is very low, the conditions are very clear, the fish are stale, and there simply isn't much doing at all, then it often pays to look around for alternatives, and one of the great beauties of Ireland is that it offers endless options for the fly fisherman. Once you realize that there isn't a fish that swims that won't take a fly of one design or another, then huge opportunities are opened up to you – providing, of course, that you appreciate that all fish have their merits, and not just those with adipose fins.

FRESHWATER OPTIONS

Let's start with the Cork Blackwater. You've got a lightweight floating-line kit with you – five-weight would be ideal, although four-weight would find favour with the connoisseur. You're going to try for dace. Yes, they may only average eight ounces and become a real trophy at double that weight, but who cares when they're as beautiful and silvery and game as these. You'll find dace in comparatively quick, streamy water that's between two and five feet deep and flushing over gravel. They'll be grouped up in large shoals, and you'll often see them rising. That's the way to hunt them, on any small dry fly that's black or grey and isn't bigger than a size 20. Rises are lightening-quick, and here's part of the excitement: if you hook five dace out of every ten rises, then you can really count yourself an expert.

NYMPH FEEDERS *Roach rely heavily on small aquatic insects for their diet and they are easily caught on small nymphs and dry flies. A one-and-a-half-pounder on a four-weight kit can give a fight to remember.*

You should consider any trip to Ireland worthwhile if you manage to land a three-pound rudd on a fly, for here is a beauty of a fish. A body like a pan of gold, and fins a crimson you thought only existed on the cover of a 1970 psychedelic pop album. You'll find rudd – and big ones – in any one of hundreds of Irish loughs scattered around the country. You're best off searching for them near to lilies and weed beds, and amongst extensive reeds. Look for shoals topping on the surface and for big, splashy rises. You're never going to get very close to a spooky shoal of big rudd so probably a six-weight outfit gives you just a little bit more casting distance. A floating line and either dries or nymphs, and you're in business.

How about perch? Ireland bristles with these glamorous, pugnacious fish. Most commonly, you'd expect to catch them on small fish-imitating lures, retrieved quite quickly close to the surface, through shallows and close to snags. However, perch are also browsers, and a second approach would be to fish a long leader with a team of nymphs and investigate the bottom thoroughly. Obviously, on most waters you stand a chance of trout as well, but who cares if you end up with a glorious mixed bag?

Which brings me on to that most delightful of Irish species of which so many game fishermen remain in total ignorance – the tench. Olive-skinned, red-eyed, and powerfully finned, the tench is an absolute delight. They are traditionally caught with

A BUCCANEER OF A FISH *Never, ever despise the perch. This is a wondrous fish, as beautiful and as brave as any creature that swims. A two-pound perch is a truly sensational fish – and easily caught on big, fish-imitating lures.*

"Tench on a fly rod as the pink mists of dawn lift: it really is an unbeatable angling experience."

DEMONIC FIGHTER *Believe me, once you've caught a mackerel on light fly gear, you will be tempted to do little else for the rest of your fishing life. And never, ever consider putting up a team of flies, because if you do catch two or, even worse, three on the same cast then it's farewell to that fine, expensive fly rod of yours. These fish are maniacs.*

bread, maggots, or sweetcorn, but as their natural diet consists almost entirely of beetles, bloodworm, shrimps, and nymphs, they are realistic targets for fly fishing. I would suggest that you should fish your imitation very close to the bottom, and that a bite indicator is almost essential. The key to catching them is identifying the takes. Hook one, though, and you'll be left in no doubt. Tench on a fly rod as the pink mists of dawn lift: it really is an unbeatable angling experience. They're the most obliging of species, too, because as they feed they'll throw up huge clusters of small, tell-tale bubbles. A Pheasant Tail nymph on a size 14 and you're in with every chance.

OFF TO THE COAST

The quiet, clear, hot conditions that destroy so much freshwater fishing in summer are exactly those that make fly rodding in the sea totally unmissable. What species are fly catchable? Well, prime targets are mackerel, mullet, pollock, and, perhaps most glamorously of all, sea bass. As for tackle, some use bonefish outfits that are designed for the job and are perfect for working through a light surf, but don't despair if you've only got typical freshwater fly-fishing tackle. A floating line is probably what you need and, for most situations, a seven- or eight-weight outfit.

Bass and pollock feed heavily on elvers, shrimps, and many types of small fish, so any fly that replicates these is likely to be taken – anything small, silvery, and edible-looking can be hit. One of the peak ways of taking bonefish in the warmer seas is on an imitation crab, and these work excellently for bass and pollock, as well as wrasse.

All the species mentioned come very close in shore indeed, so this is a search-and-find type of method. Keep your eyes open, and on many occasions you'll see the ocean boiling as mackerel or bass hammer into the prey shoals. For wrasse, pollock, bass, and mackerel, try rocky headlands. You'll also find bass off beaches, and both bass and mullet up estuaries.

What you don't want is a big wind, because this makes fly fishing physically difficult and you don't want to run the risk of tangles or injury. Moreover, a big wind can stir up the sand and make the water cloudy. Temperate conditions are much better – light winds and as clear a sea as possible. If you can get out early or stay out late, you're likely to catch more fish. The tide can be important, and it pays to check out the best times with local fishermen.

Very often you'll pick up all the species just a few yards out, often actually in the surf itself. It's better to cast short distances and make gentle approaches than to splash around and scare the fish off. For virtually all these fish you've got to work the fly quite briskly and impart a good lively action: for mullet, which are more of a browsing type of fish, small nymphs worked back slowly generally work best. Whatever species you're after, expect a good, solid thump – especially from mackerel, pollock, and bass – and then some frantic action!

Searching Out Irish Bass

Virtually all the Irish coast offers superb bass fishing, but as most of it is all but deserted, you can't rely on local advice. Here are a few tips on how to start.

- Try to get out on dawn or dusk tides when the weather is calm. You'll often see bass hunting on the surface, especially through the summer months.

- When you're actually fishing, keep your gear to a minimum – just rod, reel, leaders, and a fly box – and keep on the move. The more ground you cover, the more bass you're likely to contact.

- Bass feed on prawns, shrimps, sand eels, crabs, worms, and small fish, so look for areas where food items are likely to live.

- Big rock outcrops are favourite areas, as they provide cover and protection for the food items.

- Areas of weed attract prey and, therefore, the bass. Look also for big rock pools where food items become stranded by the falling tide. Bass will hunt these areas as the water begins to seep in again. Look for seemingly insignificant inlets between steep-sided cliffs. These are important collecting points for food items. The cliffs themselves provide cover for the bass.

- Look for shallow water – bass like warm water, and the shallows heat up more quickly. Worms thrive here, too.

- You'll need to do a lot of your searching at low tide, and it's not a bad idea to take a pencil and pad with you so that you can make a quick map of all the promising points you find.

- Always check the tide table before going out to look at a new area. Leave for high ground the very moment the tide begins to flood, and make sure that it can't cut you off. Always check your escape routes.

- Don't go out if it's wet or even drizzling. Weed and boulders can turn to glass under moisture. Avoid steep cliffs, and try not to go out alone.

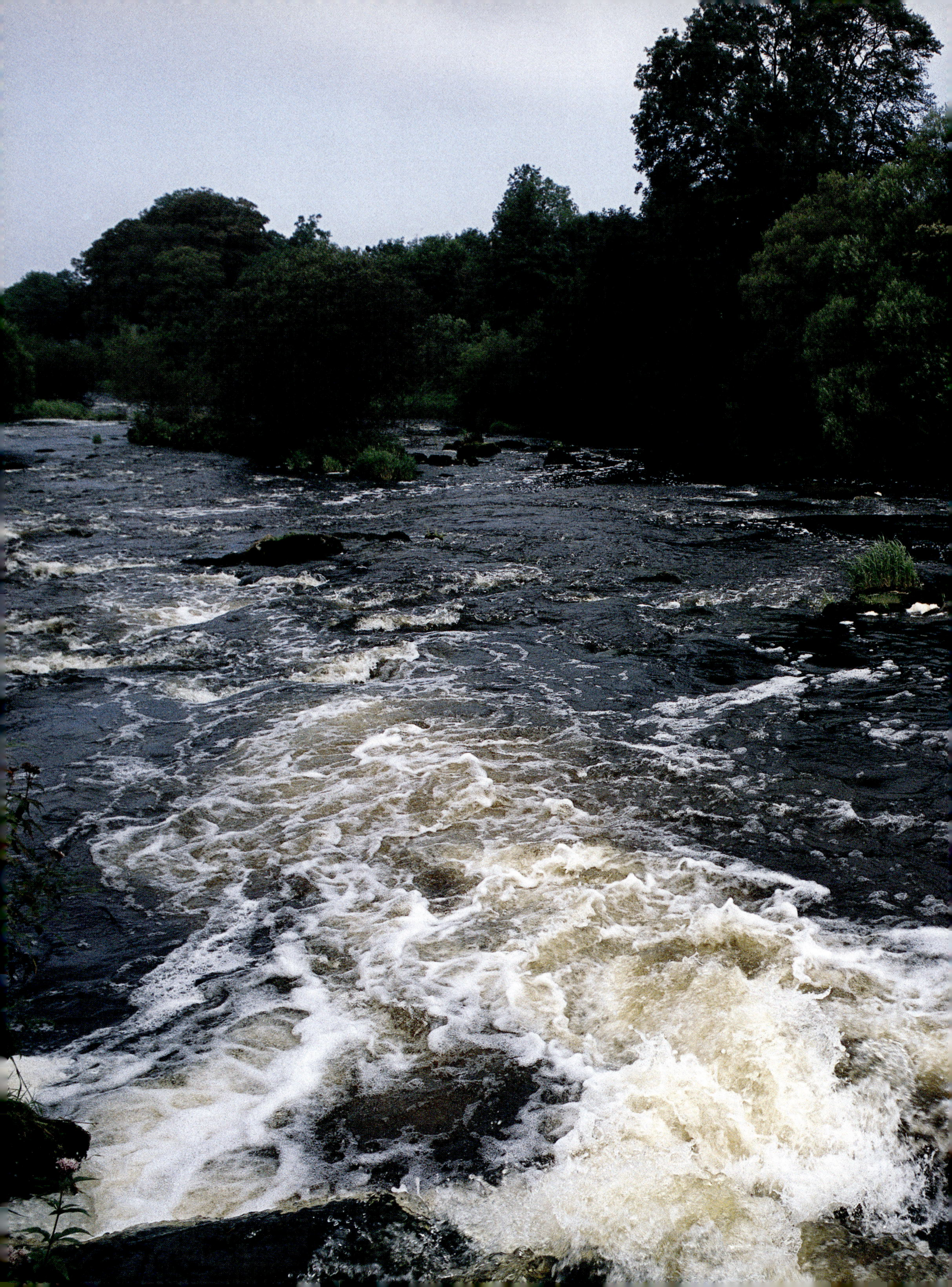

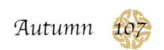

Autumn

"... for me, at least, there is absolutely nothing more thrilling than watching an artificial Daddy Longlegs disappear in a plume of water."

"Season of mists and mellow fruitfulness." Yes. Good. I don't know if Keats was an angler (I do know he spent a lot of time draped around rusted-reed winter pools), but he described Ireland's fly fishing in the autumn right enough. The days can be hot when the sun has burnt off all that Keatsian mist, and then you can expect some big flies to be about.

The autumn is the time for the Daddy Longlegs, the lumbering craneflies that give fishing almost as much excitement as the mayfly when they appear. No, I'll rephrase that: for me, at least, there is absolutely nothing more thrilling than watching an artificial Daddy Longlegs disappear in a plume of water. It's the suddenness that's exciting – the bolt out of the blue. Of course, you're expecting it to happen every minute, but that doesn't alter the fact that your heart virtually stops when it actually does. There are things you can do to quicken the process: fish on the fringe of the ripple perhaps; or just twitch the artificial from time to time so that rings radiate out, spelling lunch to the cruising brown, or salmon, come to that. Of course, you can enjoy all this same style of fishing with a big sedge, but Daddies are special.

There's an intensity about the fish through the autumn, and a lot of the fickleness of the fidgety summer months has now passed. Spawning is getting close for all of them, and this will mean death for a hefty percentage. And then, inevitably, the cold winter will follow close on autumn's heels, offering meagre rations for the survivors, so there can be little wonder that the fish look more favourably at our fur and feather in the autumn than they do in the summer salad days. Time is getting tight for them, and they know it.

Autumn is often the season for big fish, perhaps the occasional late-running salmon or sea trout, and certainly big browns that are becoming daily more aggressive as they close in on their eventual spawning sites. This is definitely a time for mercy. I think we all understand now that we don't need that life that's lying in our landing net, but that nature does. So, yes, put them back now more than at any time, and you can spend your winter smug in your righteousness.

Autumn is definitely a time to savour, for the year is now running out. Perhaps you'll wake up, look out of your window, and see a hint of frost on the lawns leading to the lough. At every gust of wind there could be a frittering of leaves. As you walk the morning river there could be drops of condensation from the overhanging alders. At this time of year, every take counts. Treat every run from every fish with wonderment, almost as though it could be your last... as well it may be, at least for the duration of the long, dark months to come.

RETURN TO ARROW LODGE
A Piker's Paradise

"Irish pike are legendary: every angler in the last 200 years has known about them."

VIRGIN WATER (opposite) *It's almost impossible to believe that in this day and age in overcrowded Western Europe there are places that you can pike fish that have probably never seen an angler before, or at least not for decades. Here, Rob fishes in the most splendid of isolation.*

MAN AFLOAT *Rob prepares to push off from the bankside, totally in control, totally fixated on the job ahead of him. This truly is an extraordinary way to explore any water.*

It's his love of wild fish and untried fisheries that has led Rob into this. We already know that Rob Maloney is a skilled trouting guide, and his knowledge of browns on Lough Arrow is unparalleled, but there are times when the lough is very difficult, when the trout are torpid and disinclined to feed, and rather than waste time, Rob would sooner be after something else. Irish pike are legendary: every angler in the last 200 years has known about them. However, the goose-gobbling monsters of the west have had a hard time of it: big fish have been taken as trophies and, with far greater effect, the Fisheries Board have netted huge numbers from loughs that they see primarily as trout preserves. Colossal fish have been removed from Mask and Corrib in particular, and so it's not to places like these that Rob takes his clients and friends. What he can show you is something uniquely special and virtually untouched.

"I would say that within half an hour's car ride of the Lodge, I could introduce you to 20 or more waters where pike can be taken on the fly," Rob says. "This is pulsating fishing. The pike are unfished for, so they're not cautious, and they're in stunning condition. Moreover, most of the loughs have hardly been fished for years, if at all, so the only footprints that you're going to see there are your own."

A Day for Alternatives

September 13th is a blissful day – warm and bright with snatches of high, fluffy cloud. The trout of Arrow will definitely be a difficult proposition, so we take to the hills. Rob's secret weapon in all this is his U-boat... a float tube that he inflates in less than a minute, straps to his back, and carries off tortoise-like across the fields. As soon as you see the water, you understand the need for this: the lake is about 10 acres in extent, and so overgrown that there's hardly anywhere to fish from the shore, certainly not with fly tackle. Rob launches himself and makes a steady circuit of the water. He casts right-handed, so he moves anticlockwise around the perimeter, casting in front of himself so he never lose sight of what his fly is doing. It's a nice, easy, and hugely efficient technique, and I bask in the sun, full of admiration. The U-boat lets him penetrate every dark, overhung corner of the water. No pike is safe, whether it be lying under branches, lilies, or deep in the recesses of fallen tree roots.

Two hours and three pike later – one of them close on 10 pounds – we're off again, to lake number two, down a lane that has a crown of wild flowers taking the place of cat's eyes along its centre. It is just possible the second lake is more beautiful than the first: it lies in a vast crater in the hills, surrounded by cliffs and forest. We pull in beside a deserted barn and walk down the slope towards it. A fox, drinking, sees us and lopes casually off. There is nobody. This is our landscape.

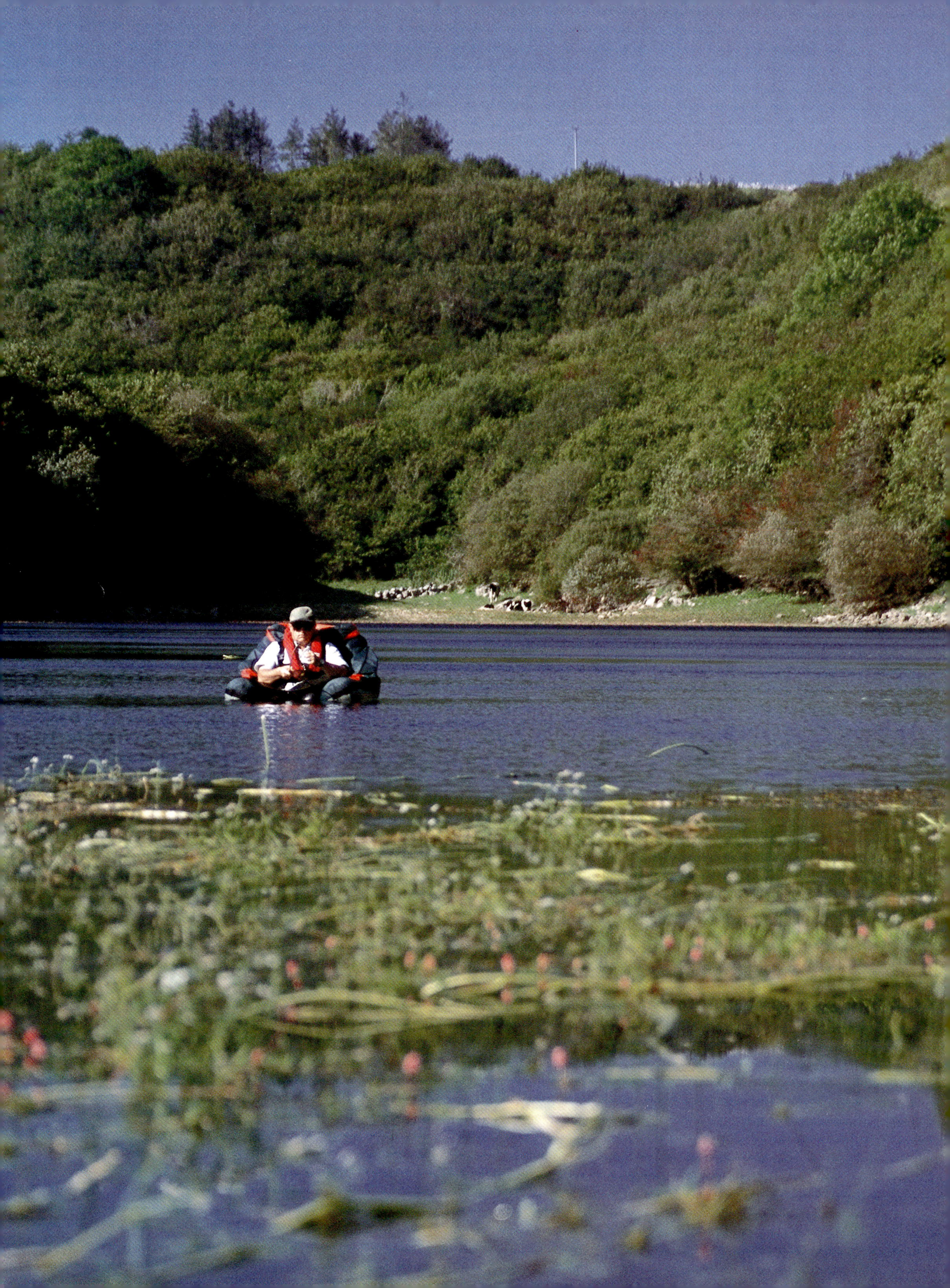

IRELAND OLD AND NEW *There's an exciting juxtaposition here between Rob and his state-of-the-art equipment and the centuries-old barn and farmyard that he's striding past towards the water. But this is Ireland – a beguiling mix of opposites that go to make such an exciting whole.*

IRISH HOSPITALITY *Fish for pike? Of course you can. What's mine is yours. This is a land where an angler with the right attitude will receive a thousand welcomes.*

Extensive shallows greet us, full of weed – and pike. At least a dozen fish arrow away from us into deeper water, and one of them is enormous. Rob flippers himself around again using exactly the same technique, and loses a very good fish indeed after some 20 minutes of battle. We never see the fish, for it stays down deep, making powerful, boring runs that indicate a very large pike indeed. Round and round Rob goes, waltzing after it, looking like a dodgem car on the rippling water. The fly comes back hopelessly mangled with the bend virtually straightened. Rob beaches to retackle and steady his nerves. "Today's a cracking day for this," he says. "The wind, especially, is crucial. You can't go out if it's over force four or five, certainly on open or rocky lakes, but there are always a few that are sheltered from the wind. I guess that I've fished 20 lakes in a tight little circle of the Lodge, but there are twice as many that I just haven't had the time to suss out. Trout, after all, are my main business, but I can really see the day when this piking begins to take over. It's just this thrill of the unknown. This fish we've just lost could have been 20 pounds, or 30, or bigger. Nobody's ever pike fished here that I know of, and that's the drug. I could dead bait for them or spin, but what's the point when I enjoy fly fishing and it's so effective? It's brilliant sport, and good, demanding, physical exercise. After you've been casting and paddling all day, your muscles really know all about it, believe me."

A Tried and Tested Method

There are good reasons why pike take flies. Over the last seven or eight years I've done a huge amount of freshwater diving, and I can tell you that the fly looks a good deal more natural in the water than the best plug, spinner, or spoon that has ever been devised. A well-tied, well-presented fly moves through the water with such fluidity, such rippling, small-fish-like grace, that you would be amazed. The feathers trap bubbles of oxygen that give the creation a lithe, lifelike look. Flashes of tinsel help, a blur of colour, feathers that look exactly like fluttering fins. When taken into the mouth, a fly feels right, too, and doesn't have the brittle hardness of a plug or spinner. Hits, then, are even more confident and, of course, when you're using a single hook the pike is much more likely to go back into the water completely unscathed. Fly fishing for pike is efficient, it's exciting, and it's conservationally kind.

And, unbeknown to many, it's traditional. Hi Regan mentions fly fishing for pike a century or more ago, and it feels as if we're going back into that era now! Our third lake of the afternoon takes some real finding, and the road leads to a lane that brings us to a track that climbs a towering hill. There's a farmhouse and the usual gang of dogs, and John, the owner, appears. We walk with him around his land, feeding his hens, praising his stock, and generally being as good as gold. "Ain't you boys wanting to fish then?" John asks us with a twinkle. "Rob, you know where the lake is by now don't you, so just get you both going!" And this lake, to my mind, is the most stunning of the three. If the others were remote, then this one is on the moon. It's also larger, perhaps 60 acres, and that in itself somehow winds up the anticipation. Again, there's not a soul around, no evidence of there ever having been anyone here – at least, not for a very long while. As we approach the lake, Rob points out the remains of an ancient crannog – a fortified island constructed in the margins many centuries ago. Pike only came to Ireland some 400 years or so ago, so crannog man would not have roasted them over his fires, but probably eels, trout, and salmon.

The sky is now wiped of cloud and the sun beams down. Bad piking conditions, but we persevere: Rob takes a fish of some eight pounds far out in the middle of the lake and I stir one of about 18 pounds close in shore, which looks twice at a large spoon and then ambles off into deeper water. Rob takes another two pike on fly while I merely have one enormous tug that comes to nought. Three nil to fur and feathers.

The End of the Day

We have promised ourselves the last of the evening on Arrow after the browns, but I sense neither of us is happy to go, Rob in particular. "I missed another big fish out there just 10 minutes ago," he moans. "The problem was, I didn't feel anything at all, so I didn't get a strike in. What you often find is that the pike will come up, take the fly, swim alongside you for a few yards, and then spit it out – and that's what happened to me just now. If I'd been surer and struck, then I'd have been in, and the

"A well-tied, well-presented fly moves through the water with such fluidity, such rippling, small-fish-like grace, that you would be amazed."

AN EYE FOR AN EYE *It should come as no surprise to anyone that fly fishing for pike is as successful as it is. It's thrilling, it's fun, and, in Ireland's unexploited waters, it's uniquely efficient.*

fish was big, no doubt. You can never quite tell what takes are going to be like. I tend to retrieve steadily, but with quite a lot of variation. Sometimes it's good just to let the fly hang, and then twitch it haphazardly. You can move the rod tip around a fair bit, too, to change direction and impart life. It's great when you can actually see the fly, because sometimes it will simply disappear with no sign of a pike at all. It's like magic. Hugely exciting. At other times, you will just get a ferocious tug and you'll be playing a fish before you even know it's on."

Most exciting of all, though, is the bow-wave take. You're pulling your fly back across comparatively shallow water when suddenly this wall of water mounts up behind it. Just one tip, though. Don't slow the fly down at this point, although it's tempting to do so. It's much better to increase the tempo and force the fish into an accelerated take, and then all hell breaks loose."

It's funny. I had thought that Lough Arrow was a wild, untamed sort of place, as indeed it is, but on our return after our day piking it looked positively homely. There were even two other boats on the water as we puttered out into the dusk. We got a couple of browns for sure, fine fish and fascinating sport, but I can tell you it was the pike that filled my dreams that night.

Piking Tips

The early part of the year can be excellent for Irish pike. If the weather in February is kind, then go for it, but March is certainly a top month. There's less weed about, and you'll find the pike coming into the shallows prior to spawning. Summer and autumn are also excellent, as the pike are active in the warmer water. Watch out for weed, however.

You don't have to float tube, but if you haven't tried it, it's thrilling sport and it certainly gets you to the very best areas. Always, however, wear a buoyancy aid, polarizing glasses, and a cap for safety. Never go out without a repair kit, either.

A nine-weight outfit is generally about right, but you might want to step up to 10-weight if the wind gets unruly. A large arbour reel is important, with a good drag system. Floating lines will do for most venues, especially when you're fishing the shallower margins. You can work a fly around three or four feet down quite easily on a floater, but you might need to go deeper if the water is tinged. You'll find the weed decays and clouds the water a little in autumn and winter, and this is when an intermediate or very slow sinking line comes into its own. Rob finds a faster sinker too much effort when he's fishing from his U-boat, although it did occur to me that a fly could be trolled effectively on water that's open and relatively snag-free.

These pike are totally unpressured, and can grow very large and fight like demons – much harder than English fish – so a 30-lb leader makes common sense, but never, ever forget to incorporate a 12- to 18-inch wire trace.

All the flies in Rob's box tend to be of the streamer variety. They're not elegant to cast, and that's one reason why you need heavier rods and lines. Rob likes to use pink-tinged flies in peat-stained water, and black ones when the sun is out and the lakes are clear. He's got a selection of barred flies to simulate small perch, which he uses around reed beds. He reckons his silver-dressed flies look like roach, but he adds touches of scarlet and gold to some to simulate rudd. Another favourite is a surface-fished fly, especially when dressed to imitate a mouse with a long, curling tail. As a last tip, man-made fibres don't look as convincing underwater as the movements of natural materials such as buck tails, sheep hair, or rabbit strips.

TAKE THE TUBE *Extraordinarily efficient as float tubing is, don't risk going out to float in a wind much above force four or five. Not only is this supremely tiring, but it could be dangerous, too.*

THE WIRE *Never, ever fish for pike on the fly without a good-sized wire trace. Twelve inches is an absolute minimum, and 18 inches is probably a good deal safer.*

A RIVER RUNS THROUGH IT
Towns on the Water

"... if it's a salmon fest that you desire, then make your way to County Sligo and the town of Ballysadare..."

We may all think that angling is a very pastoral way of passing the time, but if you want to see a salmon in Ireland – and perhaps catch one as well – then your best bet is probably to head for the towns. And if it's a salmon fest that you desire, then make your way to County Sligo and the town of Ballysadare, just to the south of the county town itself. The river is about 25 miles long, and for the last mile or so before it reaches the sea it is mouth-wateringly, excruciatingly attractive. It falls down in a series of runs, pools, and pots in a whole cavalcade of ways, all of which scream salmon, but the peculiar thing about the Ballysadare River is that until 100 years ago there were no salmon in the system whatsoever – they were instated there by one Joshua Cooper, a Victorian businessman.

The key to this strange state of affairs is the waterfall that connects the river to the sea. Its Gaelic name means "the mouth of the oak-ridged waterfall" – a rather benign sobriquet for a torrent of water that salmon find physically impossible to ascend, but it's not the force of the water coming down that defeats them. Salmon need a certain amount of depth in order to work up the momentum to power themselves along, and the shallow fall pools at Ballysadare simply don't allow them to do this. Joshua Cooper, typically of his age, saw here a fine commercial proposition going begging. He stocked the river with ova from Scotland, the nearby Moy, and even the Rhine, and then he built a fish ladder to allow the smolts back to the sea. The rest is a small part of Ireland's angling history, and you've only got to park your car, walk through the fishery, and be there at the right stage of the tide to see a phenomenon of nature.

If your arrival at Ballysadare coincides with the highest tides, you may see salmon in such numbers that you simply gawp. Many salmon ascend the fish pass, but vast numbers simply swamp the falls, raft after raft of fish pressed nose to tail up the foaming water, unable to break free into the river above. It's now that the fishery staff get amongst them, actually standing in the pools, which are more fish than water, netting them and helping them over the last, insurmountable obstacles. The remainder are physically pushed back over the ledges and into the sea to await their turn.

TIME AND TIDE...

Everything depends on tide and season: fishing begins in March with a small run of a few hundred big spring salmon, but it's when the massive run of grilse and summer salmon arrives that Ballysadare comes into its own, and when the fresh fish reach the lowest part of the pool on the rising tide, life here becomes frantic. The taste of fresh water intoxicates them, and you'll see salmon jumping, slipping, and slithering over the barely-covered rocks. The locals use a single fly on a sink tip line, knowing that a

ONE OF MILLIONS (opposite) *It's impossible to compute how many millions of salmon have run through Galway city over the centuries. Sometimes the river has seemed like a moving escalator of fish, such is the fecundity of this extraordinary fishery.*

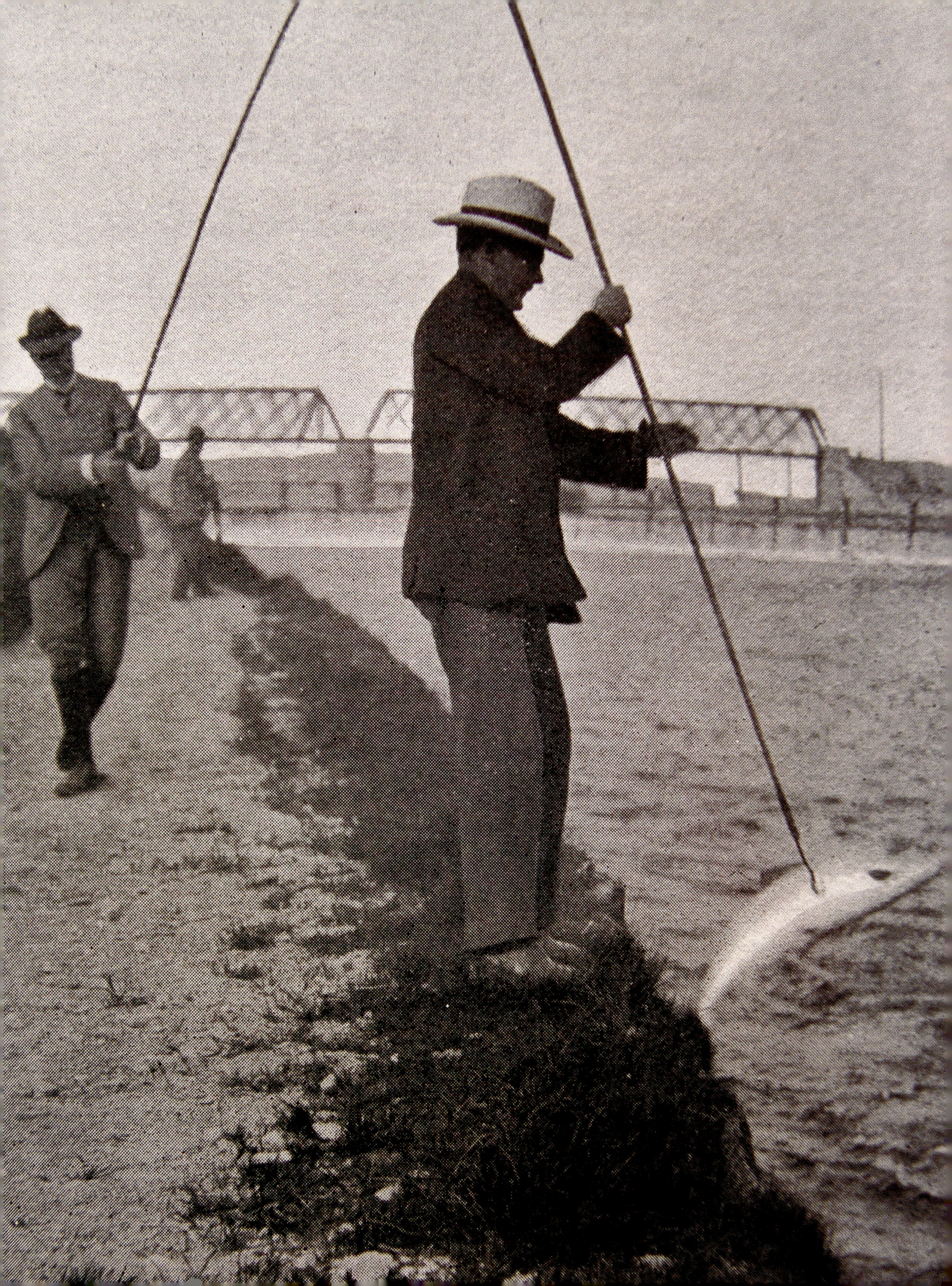

RUSH HOUR *If it's peace and quiet you're looking for on the town stretch of the Moy, then simply forget it. Here you are very much on show and fishing is nowhere more a spectator sport than here.*

FRIENDS FROM ABROAD *A visiting Italian angler snakes out a lovely line as the water is beginning to rise and the fish move. Now there's a buzz of expectation in the air. Action is about to happen.*

floater just skates across the surface but that anything fished too deep simply leads to a succession of foul-hooked fish. You might think that so many fish in such a small area would lead to sport about as exciting as shooting ducks in a barrel, but you'd be wrong. You have to fish hard and you have to fish skilfully, and about an hour before high tide the fishing comes to a complete halt as the salmon refuse to take in water that is becoming ever more salty. You won't see any locals fishing the falls now, but wait for the tide to fall and back they come. This is when panic faces the fish: do they try the weir one more time or do they drop away back into the sea? Now, for two hours, the fevered fish are at their most vulnerable, and it is believed that when the water level drops to the lowest rung of the fish ladder most salmon are caught.

This is a magnificently run fishery, welcoming and with a host of fish-friendly rules. Many of the fish are small – under six pounds – but this should be of no consequence: to see such a frenetic example of nature's vibrancy is exciting enough.

A Public Spectacle

I've got to take you back a little bit now to the high summer and a blisteringly hot Saturday afternoon. Galway city is a mass of shoppers, the streets jammed with cars inching through between the packed pavements. The bars are full to overflowing and there's a festive atmosphere all around. Down by the cathedral the Galway River flows, and its banks are packed with people of all kinds – picnickers, walkers, tourists, shoppers, students. Scores of them stop on the road bridge and hang over, peering into the bright, clear water beneath. There seem to be salmon everywhere and, a little way upstream, on the left-hand bank as I look, there's a fisherman – fast into a fish.

This is a scene that Hi Regan, one of Irelands' most beloved of authors, avoided like the plague, preferring the rural peace of the lough and the river, but the man whom I and a thousand others are watching doesn't care. He can't hear the traffic or the cries of the crowd, and he's not longing for the lonesome moor. He's far too intent for that. This salmon, at this moment, is his entire focus on the world – perhaps the more so because he's clearly no expert.

In truth, the salmon is making something of a mockery of him: there's loose fly line around his feet threatening to trip him up at any moment, and he's failing to keep anything like proper contact with the fish. Sometimes he's playing it far too hard, and at other times there's barely a bend in the rod. It's a miracle that the fly is still lodged in the scissors. For a long while now the salmon has been virtually beneath me, holding its own against the push of water around the parapet. The angler is neither coming down the bank towards the fish nor is he trying to walk it upstream, and it's something of a stalemate. We can only watch the fish as its muscular form fights both the current and the varying degrees of tension the angler is exerting, and there's something exhilarating and vital about the scene. The fish is fighting for a life that is desperately precious. That streamlined shape, so muscular and so lithe, seems to cut through the water like a sword whenever it decides to make a move. Its agility, its balance, the thrust of its tail, the obvious power of its fins all proclaim it to be a master of its own particular universe – unlike the floundering fisherman now lathered in sweat and, by the look on his face, close to sobbing under the strain of it all.

Two locals are on the path beside him now, trying hard to help. They get him to walk towards the fish, pumping up line as he goes. All that slack that was collecting gravel and dirt at his feet is now on the spool, and the rod has a healthy bend. The fish beneath me is much more agitated now as it senses the growing menace. It is higher in the water, making the surface boil and heave. It thrashes itself clear a couple of times, foaming the water and drawing gasps from the crowd. It's as fresh as new-laid snow, its belly just as white, an eight-pound fish, very probably just in from the bay. My favoured outcome is a hard one to call: this could well be the angler's first salmon, and to lose it now after being so close would be a tragedy for him. If this fish breaks free it will leave a wound that will never truly be healed. I know that only too well, but this fish, this glorious, sleek, silver salmon responding to nature's deepest, most impulsive commands – how can you wish it anything but luck during such a short life of chance and danger? It's impossible to decide, and I'm tempted to go back into the town, buy some film, have a coffee, and try to forget the whole thing.

THE LURE OF THE WEIR *Every angler loves a weir – the oxygen, the sights, the sound, and always the hope of a salmon wriggling and thrashing its way towards its destiny.*

ONE IN A LINE *It might not seem the rural idyll we think angling to be, but there's an excitement here in Ballina, a feeling that this is the place to be and that you miss out on it at your peril... and when the fish are running, you're quite correct.*

"You might be quiet, you may be shy, but you've got to experience urban fishing like this just once in your life..."

"Give him some slack!" "Play him hard or he'll be under the bridge!" "Keep his head up, don't let him get back in the main flow!" – calls that must have resounded thousands of times over the years around one of the most intense and public fisheries in the world. I know that millions of salmon have been dispatched from the Galway Fishery, and I wonder at my squeamishness. Beside me, a Chinese girl is clapping feverishly, her eyes all a-dazzle with excitement. A French family is cheering madly – the fish is on its side now on a short line and the end cannot be far off. So that's it then, I'll be off to the town.

But wait: one of the Galway men has the salmon by the belly, down there in the shallows. He's looking up to the angler and it's rather like the Coliseum when the crowd waited for the turn of the Emperor's thumb – and it's thumbs up today! The fly falls away at the sudden release of pressure, and those Galway hands rock the fish for a second or two in the margins. Slowly, free and bewildered, the salmon noses its way back into the flow and, with a flourish of that tail, is gone in a flash of light.

BALLINA ON THE MOY

Of all the towns in Ireland, and very conceivably in the world come to that, there's none that so obviously has a fishing river running through it as Ballina, at the mouth of the River Moy in County Mayo. The town fishery is a phenomenon, and its 10-year average reveals almost two-and-a-half thousand fish per season. It is superbly run under the management of the North Western Regional Fisheries Board. The Ridge Pool, the Cathedral beat, Ash Tree Pool, Spring Wells, the Point, and the Polnamonagh all offer some of the most exciting Atlantic salmon fishing in the world.

But it's intense. As in Galway, you're under public scrutiny and your ability will be assessed in seconds. The chances are there will be a dozen anglers sitting on the wall behind you watching how you cast, how you mend the line, how you work your fly, and how you lean into your fish. You'd think every resident of Ballina was an expert – even the old lady coming out of the Post Office with her pension has an opinion.

Of course, the Moy is hugely prolific upstream, away from Ballina. The Mount Falcon Fisheries, Attymass, Armstrongs, Foxfords, the Cloongee, and the East Mayo Fishery all offer superb sport in more serene surroundings, but the hustle and bustle of Ballina town is irresistible. Again, everything depends on the tide. When the river is low and dead there may well be salmon flopping around and visitors fishing hard, but you won't find the locals out. Once the river begins to rise or fall, then it's a different matter altogether. The bailiffs become animated. The walkie-talkies begin to buzz. Fish show everywhere and the town takes an interest. It's now that all the rods are taken up, and if you stand on any one of the bridges you'll see a line of anglers upstream and down thrashing the river for every ounce that it's worth. You might be quiet, you may be shy, but you've got to experience urban fishing like this just once in your life for the adrenaline buzz alone. You may well find it addictive.

FLY FISHING ON THE RIVER MOY

Much of the Moy consists of very deep, very slow pools, and you have to accept that there's a lot of worming and spinning. However, between these areas there is endless water for the fly fisherman and, because there are so many different depths and current speeds to contend with, there's a rare opportunity to experiment with different methods of working the fly and trying out different patterns.

The Moy demands a variety of lines. You'll need floating lines for the shallower, quicker runs, but various sink tips play their part in low and soft rising water. You'll need a sinking line when there's a big push of fresh water on during a rising flood, before the water starts to colour too much for the fly.

You can get away with a 9- or 10-foot single-handed rod using trout flies as small as size 16 in very clear, low conditions.

Shrimp flies are essential – the John Anthony shrimp on a number 14 treble is a favourite. However, Moy salmon are notoriously fickle and it pays to take as many patterns, sizes, and colours as your fly box can accommodate.

Don't forget to include a good mayfly selection too, as grilse especially will come up to flies on the surface.

Local advice stresses the importance of fly action. Impart as much as you reasonably can, but slow down the speed at which it moves through the water. It's also important to get the depth of the fly right and work it along the levels where the salmon are hanging.

Finally, don't ignore the deep, apparently lifeless pools best reserved for the spinning angler. Cast a long sinking line across the river and retrieve the fly at varying speeds through the 10- to 16-foot depth zone. Bear in mind that you can catch fish anywhere along the river on the fly providing the water isn't too coloured.

THE MARCH OF THE SALMON *It's possible on the Moy to look down from any one of the bridges and see salmon lined up like soldiers waiting to ascend. It's a thrilling sight, and it's very reassuring to discover that in these difficult environmental times there are still oases of natural plenty.*

LOUGHS CONN AND CULLIN
Healy's Hotel

"... the place itself has the true feel of a fishing hotel. There are rooms here that old Isaak would have approved of..."

CULLIN AT DUSK (opposite) *A magic time. The rudd shoals are dimpling. Big trout are coming up for sedges. The boats rock at anchor, impatient to be out in the action.*

HEALY'S HEAVEN *Can there be a more beautiful fishing hotel in the world, never mind in Ireland? This is a little bit of Paradise sheltered from the outside world.*

"Healy's Hotel? I can think of no better place for an angler," my old friend Gordon Heath told me as I left his cottage, quite confident of my next destination, for in the 17 years that I've known Gordon he's never been wrong. The moment you see Healy's you appreciate its lovely, ever-changing view of Lough Cullin, small sister lake to the vast Conn, and, sure enough, the place itself has the true feel of a fishing hotel. There are rooms here that old Isaak would have approved of: the sheets may not actually smell of lavender, but there are boats rocking in the bay, just across the lawn from the building and, above all, the hotel bar is the meeting place for the very best of guides from far and wide.

I met my host, Graham Williams, in the hotel hallway within minutes of my arrival, but it was all a bit of a fluster. Graham, you see, was trying to breathe life into a bat that had fallen into the lough near his boat earlier. To my unpractised eye, it seemed as though the bat was on the mend: its fur seemed perky and its ears were all a-twitch – surely signs of a bat raring to go? Graham's face, however, was creased in concern. Would it survive? Would it be able to catch its fly feast and pump its own energy into this tiny quivering body? Shouldn't we give it a drop or two of sugared water? Should it be put up in the eaves of a barn? Or should it be taken to recover in a ruin on the lake's island? In the meantime, we let it rest awhile on a bench in the beer garden, and I tried to get a little more information.

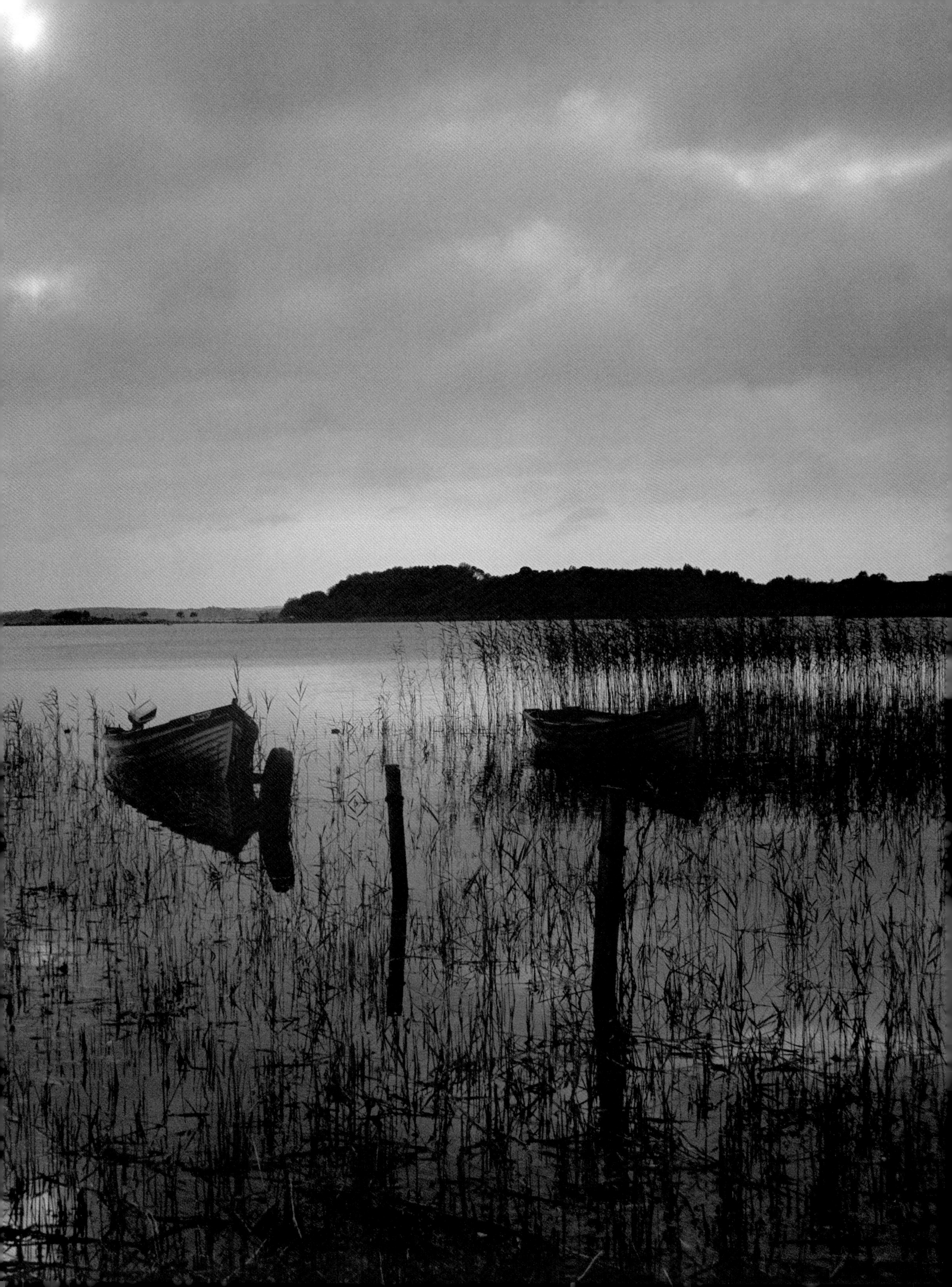

SALMON STREET *The channel between Loughs Conn and Cullin is one of the most celebrated of all salmon hotspots in Ireland. When the fish are on the run, this place is a magnet to those in the know.*

Love At First Sight

Graham, it appeared, had been a director of the satirical Spitting Image TV programmes, but he became sick of the rules and the restrictions. Visiting his Irish girlfriend and revelling in the area of Conn, he came to love the fishing more and the travelling less. Pilgrimages up the M11 to Stansted airport were only bearable as part of a journey to a way of life that was increasingly casting its spell. The people, the pace, the whole feel of rural Ireland was getting to Graham, making his London-based, high-pressure life increasingly impossible for him. Then, one fateful day, he came round a bend in the road, saw Healy's and a cluster of cottages, and knew this is where he had to live. Easy as that – or so he makes it sound.

With the typical Williams gusto that I came more and more to appreciate, Graham made his decision, upped sticks and moved across the water. Of course, he needed a job and he wanted to guide, but he was careful to tread gently in such a small, tight community. It took time to learn from the other guides, to get his own boat, to experiment by himself for long stretches of time on the lake. Then he began to ghillie in competitions, provided that every single one of the local guides was already employed and he could be sure he wasn't taking an Irishman's livelihood. Little by little, Graham became accepted and, 10 years on, he has become one of the brothers.

I must say he was so worried about the bat that evening that it was hard to get Graham to talk, but we finally put it into the high branches of a hedge where it sat for a while contemplating the twilight. Then, in a whirl of wings, it was away, piping over the reeds and the water, happy to be home. Graham turned to me with a triumphant smile, and this on the face of a man who would once have destroyed the career of a politician in the time it takes to hit out a fly line. Here is a man who has found his true happiness, I guessed – rightly.

"Look," he said. "I've got to go now. I've got an evening gig. (Guiding sessions in Graham speak are always gigs.) I won't be back until late, but let's meet up in the bar tomorrow morning over a coffee and I'll fill you in with everything you need to know."

"Little by little, Graham became accepted and, 10 years on, he has become one of the brothers."

124 Loughs Conn and Cullin

THE WORLD STANDS STILL *Ireland isn't simply exquisite for the big picture. Look at the details. Absorb the little things, and you will better form an impression of this whole, stunning other world.*

PAST GLORIES *If a trout is not to be released, then a glass case is not a bad resting place for it. The capture of a good trout can be one of the high spots of anyone's life: it's good to be able to reel in the years and savour that excitement again.*

From the Horse's Mouth

The night was blissfully quiet, with just the chop of the wind on the lough outside the window, and I was in good heart to meet up with Graham again, and with Gerry Murphy, the admiral of the local boat hire fleet. We sat in the sun-drenched window of the bar, a map of Cullin and Conn stretched out before us.

"Cullin is the most dangerous of the big lakes," Graham said. "It's shallow, with a huge number of rocks, and in a wind it can be treacherous. You really do need a guide. It's a lake to be fished early. It heats up faster than Conn and gets its mayfly fix earlier. I've got my diary here. Oh, how about that? The first cuckoo on 19th April, the mayfly up on May 1st exactly, and the big fish found them around 7th or 8th May, according to this. Any Wulff pattern will do. Grey, green, yellow, just the bog standards. Our best day was 10 boats out with 20 anglers and 58 fish kept, with at least double that number put back. Eighteen of those fish were over three pounds and there were lots just under. The trouble is that Cullin does get fed by the river from Castlebar, and that brings a lot of muck in. Combine that with the shallowness of the water and the heat of the summer, and it becomes a water too weedy to fish by June or July. It's then we move onto Conn."

Gerry shuffled the map round so that I could see Conn more clearly. I noticed his hands were big and strong from a lifetime of rowing. He jabbed a finger at the sea of blue. "Conn is a big water, 12 miles long, so where do you start, even with a guide? We all of us like Coleman's Shallows, but this can get a pounding because it's so close to Gillaroo Bay and so sheltered from the wind – easy to access and easy to fish, you see. Massbrook Point to Victoria Bay is a good reach for the salmon. The water is six to eight feet deep and it's over a bottom of sand, stone, and shingle, which is what the fish seem to like, but it gets trolled a lot, so that can make them shy. This year there were a huge number of fish there from June onwards, because big rain had pushed them right up the River Moy and they just kept on going. We had six fish in a single day, one of them on a size 14 Black Gnat and an eight-and-a-half-foot rod. I've never done so much rowing after a fish in all my life."

"That's right," Graham added. "You've got to remember, John, it's all seasonal. You keep your ear to the water, as it were. As soon as Cullin goes off, then you look to the north end of Conn – areas like Bog Bay and Castle Hill Bay. They come on because they are some of the shallowest parts of the water and warm up fastest. Castle Hill Bay is also a prime mayfly ground, because it's surrounded by vegetation and the air can be just thick with them. As these areas go off, you find Poteen Island begins to come on, along with Sandy House Bay. It's a short drift, but it can be really productive. Another great drift is around Glass Island, and it doesn't matter how the wind comes at you there because you can go in any direction. School House and Six Arches Bay also hit at the time Poteen's at its height. I've had some great gigs out there."

"And don't forget the river stretch that links Conn and Cullin," Gerry said, pointing my gaze just a handful of miles from the hotel. "You've got 400 yards of totally free water here that every salmon has to pass through at some stage or another. No wonder it gets hammered. It can be like an NCP car park here, with more floats and spinners being hurled about than you've ever seen in your life. It wasn't long ago the fisheries people put out rumours of big catches of salmon. They waited until 6.30 on a Saturday morning, did a raid, and collared 50 people for fishing without licences. Sure saved the bailiffs some travelling time, eh?"

"You've got a chapter to write, John," Graham said. "So the information I'd give is that if people have to book a holiday in advance, go for the last two weeks in May and the first in June. June is perhaps the better of the periods, because the trout are more used to finding the mayfly by that stage. When it all begins, you see loads of mayfly and no fish. By June you could catch them on a Rizla fag paper! It's interesting that there's not as much dapping on Conn as there is on Corrib, but it really does work. I've got to say that August is generally the deadest month. It's the start of the fry feeding, and if the trout are on perch fry, especially, they're much less likely to come up for dry or wet flies. You can still get good fish, though, and we had a cracker last month that fell for an artificial Daddy and still had four perch fry, all alive, in its mouth. Really, though, it doesn't matter what you're catching. It's just a gem of a place to be. Anyway, you're coming out with me this afternoon aren't you, so we can talk a bit longer then. I've got a gig on now, but I do know John wants a quick word with you before we go out."

WHERE THERE'S A WILL...

John Dever describes himself as the Castlebar kid who became rich and ploughed a million pounds into Healy's to turn its fortunes around. "I've felt angry half my life at what's been done around here. I'm a local lad, but I've got the ability to see the sin

VOLATILE WATERS *You need to be aware that even massive lakes such as Conn and Cullin are at the mercy of the elements and heavy rains can swell them. This is especially important for the boat fisherman, as vicious rocks can be hidden by just a skim of water.*

THE PLAN UNFOLDS *With such a large water as Conn, it's not a bad idea to get a map out, consider the prevailing wind on the day, and make plans accordingly – bearing in mind, of course, that in Ireland plans are only made to be changed...*

THE TEACHER IN ACTION *This is Graham doing what he does best – imparting his vast knowledge, not only of the lough but of how best to fish it. He's a natural teacher, and his guidance comes over warmly and with generosity of spirit.*

and the stagnation of the past. Look closely at that map of Graham's. See how huge the drainage system of Conn and Cullin is? Every little ditch and stream eventually finds its way into them. And they're like so many furred arteries leading into a clogged heart. There have been so many problems in the past you hardly know where to start looking: the sewage plants at Castlebar and Crossmolina; all the fertilizer spread on the land; the slatted cattle sheds and the seeping slurry tanks – when it's been too wet to spread it on the land then they've simply dumped it into the rivers. And where does all this muck eventually ended up? In Conn and Cullin, of course, and the effect I needn't bother telling you about. It's just a miracle of God that the lakes still produce so many fish of such a high standard.

"But I believe in a proactive approach. I like to tell the truth. I'm not afraid of speaking out to get things done. We're not going to sit back quietly and let these gems go the way that places like Sheelin did. We're getting the wheels moving. It's all change at the Castlebar sewage plant. The Government's making farmers tow the line – they need a licence now to empty slurry tanks, and there are spot checks. There are also questions being asked about the amount of fertilizer they buy and where they are going to use it. As far as I'm concerned, I'd take just about any action to get these loughs right again, but they're on their way. That third week in May proved that. Graham's already told you how we just couldn't stop catching fish. Things couldn't continue in the old ways and the tide is definitely turning. We're getting our loughs back, and although they're good now, they'll be brilliant soon."

ON THE DRIFT

Fishing the traditional drift style on a large lough in a friendly breeze can be one of fishing's most liberating experiences. It is one of the ultimate expressions of going with the flow, and when you have great companions you'll spend not a second of your life in a better way. Graham picks me up around about 2pm and on board are Cullin, his fishing dog friend, and a Swede we'll call Sven, although we never did quite decipher his name.

There are those who would say that our drift was not one to be treasured… Graham puts up my delight of a lough rod and happens to break the tip in two as he pulls the line through the rings. We replace it with Gerry's best outfit, which must have been designed at clown school. Charles Jardine? Lee Wulff? The fisher has yet to be born who could feather down a cast with Gerry's rod. Graham tries half a dozen times, reddens, and takes to the oar. I try twice, sense Cullin looking at me, head cocked in despair, and I catch Graham's eye. We double up with laughter. Gerry, bless his heart, isn't a purist is he? It's easy to tell he wasn't brought up on the Itchen. We examine the line. It's a weight forward with the forward bit cut off, but worse is to come. As we fool around with Gerry's outfit, Sven finds the wine and drinks it. Add to this a break in the cloud cover and a dropping wind, and we all agree that we're stumped.

But you never know. Sometimes, just sometimes, a monster comes out of the deep to make the reel sing, or croak in the case of Gerry's, and out on Conn it's easy to get lyrical when you see the sun light up the clouds and shafts of light dance on the water – all absolute, unmarred beauty.

It's the salmon that are making the drift perfect for me. Has there been a minute out of the past 40 when we haven't seen one or heard one jump? How do they make that noise as they enter air space? You can actually hear them leave the water long before you hear the thump of their re-entry. Cullin is aquiver, typical of the best type of fishing dog who is more a part of the team than, dare I say it, Sven? The dog is all alertness. He whines and moans as an eight-pound salmon flops out 20 yards from the boat. I haven't got a clue why the salmon are here in such outrageous numbers.

"Look down," Graham tells me. My gaze follows his pointing hand to the water in front of the boat and down through a curtain of daphnia. The water is four feet deep, six at the most, and it's all sandy gravel for thousands and thousands of yards. This is perfect salmon water in any lough. Of course, there's no chance of catching one, and Graham doesn't care. Sven, looking at his last glass of Pinot Noir, doesn't seem concerned either. But Cullin cares. After all, he's a guiding spaniel, and spectacular sunsets mean bonio-all to him! And, all of a sudden, I care.

Totally out of nowhere, a salmon of around six pounds comes up to the surface film and mooches around my sedge drowning there. For three seconds he hangs close, long enough for him to see it and for us all to see him. We watch him shrug his darkening shoulders and cruise on his way. Cullin whines and barks. Graham is saying "Sit!" (at least, I think that's what he said). I'm still agog with excitement, my heart racing, knowing full well why a drift, even an unpromising one like this, is to be treasured. "Fantastic," says Sven. "Such body these Aussie wines."

SUNSET SATISFACTION *Can there be a better moment than the end of the day when the breezes die away, the sun sinks, and the light takes on its mellow, golden hue? Then the big fish come up for the hatching sedges or the buzzers and, at last, after a hard day they're uniquely vulnerable.*

BEATEN *A trout lies in surrender in the bankside grasses. It's now your choice. Is he for the breakfast table or does he return to grow larger and wiser?*

MELVIN and THE ERNE
Sonaghan, Gillaroo, and Sea Trout

"I had a blinder of a day with him last year out on Lough Melvin, and I was hugely impressed."

By common consent, you can't get a better guide to the Melvin and Erne region than Jim Dillon, a captain in the Irish army and a real commander of the fishing hereabouts. Everyone had told me that Jim was the man to see but, coincidentally, I met up with Jon Ward Allen of *Waterlog* magazine the day before our appointment. "Captain Jim! Well how about that? I had a blinder of a day with him last year out on Lough Melvin, and I was hugely impressed. It was a very difficult day, and a number of guides would have given up, especially considering my lack of ability and my lackadaisical attitude. Not Jim. He was really focused, and deeply wanted me to catch a fish. I have to admit, I was keen to see one of these sonaghan, and when eventually we got one, it was purely down to Jim's skill and perseverance. A great day." And what a great a testimonial!

Helping people is the essence of Jim's life, whether he's in uniform or afloat. He is lean, hugely agile, heavily tanned and, when I met him, just back from Eritrea. Jim is a living embodiment of what a member of the world's new armies should be. Out in Africa, Jim had been working on a peace mission, trying to put together a shattered society suffering from chronic poverty, disease, lawlessness, and political breakdown. AIDS is rampant there, rocking the very foundation of all life. "Even training people is a difficulty," Jim said. "If you take on 10 Eritreans, by the time you have trained them up the chances are four of them will have died. It's a dreadful, wasteful situation for a country and a people to be in, and my heart bleeds. All we can really do is keep the peace and do our best for them."

MASTER OF ALL (opposite) *Jim Dillon surveys the shore and the estuary, contemplating the chances of sea trout success. Jim, a captain in the Irish army, knows the importance of preparation, and these wide open, untapped waters excite his imagination.*

A VIEW OF THE DROWSE *There are those who think of the Drowse as manufactured and artificial, but that's not always the case. There are places where it remains as lovely as any salmon river in Ireland – and certainly one of the most productive.*

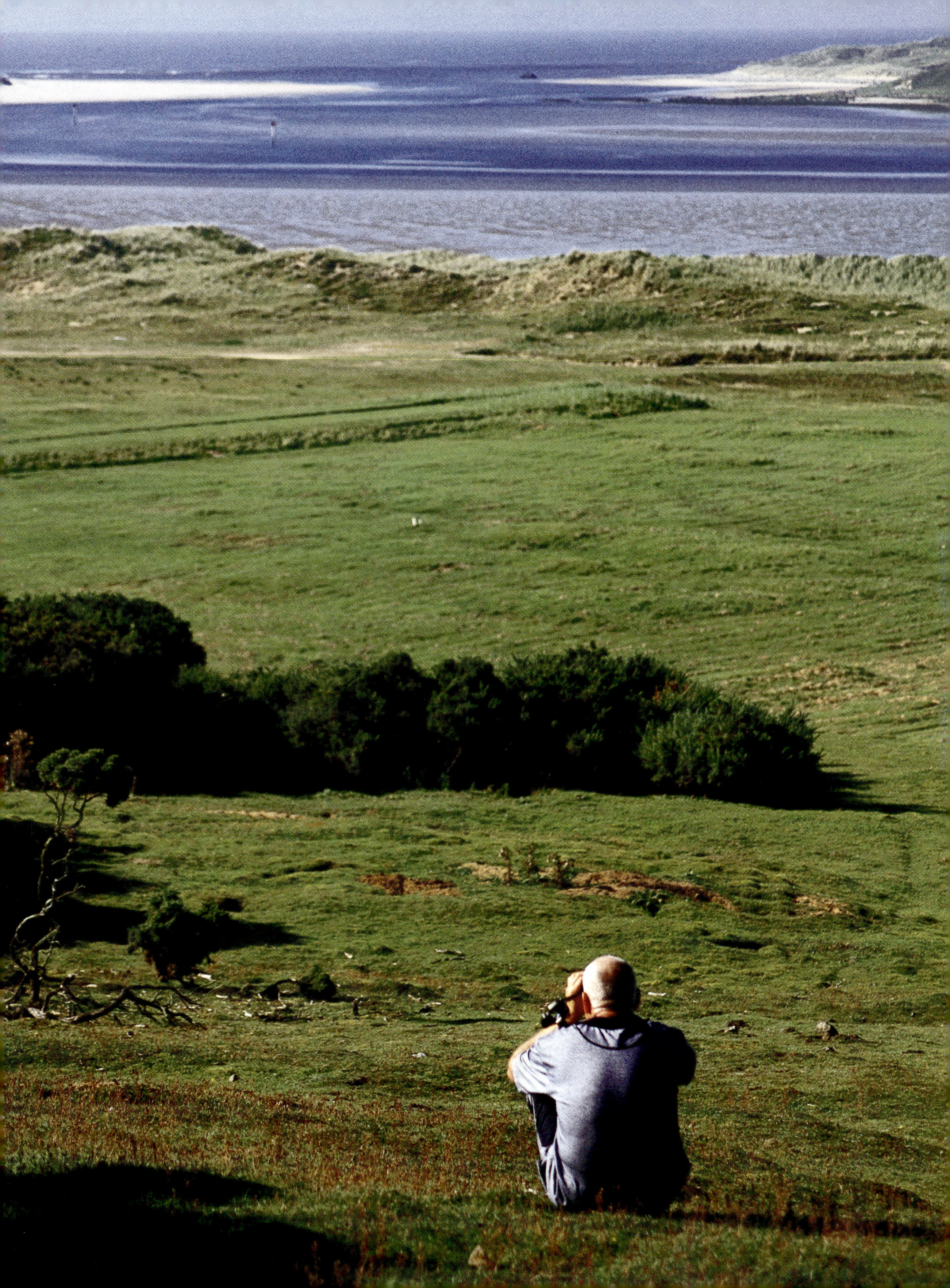

THE ESTUARY *There's something uniquely compelling about fishing an estuary. It's all about the shift of the tide and the coming and going of the fish, waltzing in such close harmony to the moon-driven movements of the waters themselves.*

Just as he was doing with his kids. His wife was away on holiday and Jim was deputizing, running the family as well as the guiding business and the guesthouse, all with apparent aplomb. Once everyone was settled, we took a coffee and sat out in his garden, poring over maps of the area.

The Sonaghan of Melvin

"It's a great region for the fisherman here," Jim said, scanning the map. "You've obviously got Lough Melvin, which is prime, but don't forget Lough Erne and the Drowse River. There are some fascinating hill loughs, too, but I'll come to those later. I suppose Melvin is at the top of your interest list, just as it is for most people, largely because of our two constant star attractions – the sonaghan and the gillaroo. There are normal browns, of course, and ferox and salmon in the lough, but it's the first two that seem to fascinate everybody.

"There are plenty of sonaghan in the lough, and they probably average about 11 inches in length. A one-and-a-half-pound fish is quite unusual. What is special about them is that they look rather like sea trout – long, slim, and silver – and they fight dramatically hard for their size. They're real live wires. For long spells, they're daphnia feeders, and so where the banks of daphnia are, there you'll find the sonaghan. It should be as simple as that! The usual rules apply. If it's bright, you'll find the daphnia down deep, just as you would after heavy rain, which also pushes them below. Better days are therefore cloudy and dull, when the daphnia rise and the fish follow. I tend to use intermediate or sink tip lines with a selection of flies – the Clan Chief, the Bibio, the Octopus, the Golden Olive Bumble, Claret Hoppers – flies that are subdued in colour, but still have a bit of flash about them. You're best off fishing quite short and retrieving quickly. Takes are electrifyingly quick, and you can miss one after another if you're out on a long line. I've seen people miss 40 takes on the bounce and never get near a fish. If you're not in complete contact, forget it. Don't be in too much of a hurry to take your flies out at the end of the retrieve, but dibble them close to the boat. Sonaghan will often follow in right to the last few feet. They can be such tricky fish beneath the surface, it's almost a relief when September comes along and you can get them up top on grasshopper imitations.

"There's a huge array of areas that we guides head for. Larean Bay is good early on, as it has shallow water that warms up quickly. From mid-May, we go out over deeper water. Farrells Bay to Roosky Point is good, and we try out Bilberry Island and Schoolhouse Bay."

THE GILLAROO

"For gillaroo, you need to look for rocky areas – the shores around islands are always good. They fish best after a bit of stormy weather, when the bottom is really stirred up and the food items that they hunt for are exposed. That really gets them going. You need to get right into the rocks, so you want a boatman with a bit of skill. You've got to get deep down to them, as well, because they rarely feed very far off the bottom. The gillaroo has a gizzard like a chicken and feeds extensively on snails, so there's a clue to fly patterns. It's a beautiful fish – the spotting is absolutely amazing – but don't expect the fight you get from a sonaghan. They tend to stay deep, and they don't do anything particularly dramatic. They're bigger than the sonaghan though – you'll pick up the odd two-pounder and, exceptionally, you'll find them getting up to three pounds, or even four. Mind you, it's the fish of a lifetime at that size. Very occasionally you will come across the char, and there are lots of those as well, some quite good ones. and because we've got char, it follows that there are ferox, too. These average between five and eight pounds and are quite prolific."

We took a short break. Jim had children to look after and a guest was just checking in. I sat for a while, browsing through the captain's battery of fly boxes. A career in the army, a reputation as one of Ireland's top guides, a guesthouse, a family, and still the time for all this fly tying! Jon is right: there is a lot of focus about this man.

"All the attention seems to be on Lough Melvin," Jim continued. "It's a shame, because Lough Erne is fishing really well these days. It could be something to do with the zebra mussels that have got into the system. They've filtered out the suspended

"Takes are electrifyingly quick, and you can miss one after another if you're out on a long line."

TREASURE ISLAND *On the biggest waters, such as Lough Erne, islands are always magnets for fish. Work them closely and carefully and you're always in with a chance.*

particles that used to make the water dirty, and now it's crystal clear. Before the zebra mussels, you could only really catch the browns from Erne on the top during the mayfly season, but now the fishing is cracking throughout the year. The mayfly is still good and runs right through to the end of July, and after that you can bring them up to sedge imitations. It's not particularly fast fishing, especially after the mayfly, but you can still bring in four really good fish a day. Erne is a huge lake, and I'd recommend trying the islands and bays to the west of Eagle Island itself. If more people fished Erne, they'd realize just what huge potential it offers. It's so big and so rich, and the trout are averaging pretty near a pound and a half in weight. It's magnificent stuff all right."

THE FLY AND THE FISHERMAN *This beautiful creature settled on my notebook as I wrote, as though intent upon inspecting my scrawled words.*

Sea Trout in the Erne Estuary

I'm keen for Jim to talk about the Drowse, the river that runs from Melvin and that is legendary for its salmon but, to be frank, I can see that Jim isn't overly keen. I guess that with all the wild, challenging fishing that Ireland offers there's something perhaps a tad twee about the fishery with its wooden walkways and gravelled car parks. It was quite evident that Jim much preferred to talk about the sea trout on the Erne estuary, a type of fishing that's really getting Ireland buzzing these days. Anglers of the calibre of Peter O'Reilly, Alan Pearson, Roy Williams, and Judd Ruane have made great headway with tackle, tactics, and flies. Jim himself is in the first, pioneering wave of anglers, and you can tell this is something very close to his heart.

So we upped sticks, folded up our maps, took our coffee cups back into the kitchen, and set off northwards from Jim's base in Bundoran, a short hop up the coast towards Ballyshannon. We turned off before the town and wandered over the fields that offer a good view of the Erne estuary itself, and what a beautiful place it is – wide-open spaces, eternal skies, and a tantalizing blue vein of river snaking its way to the sea.

"We're talking about a wildly unpredictable type of fishing here, and I think all of us are still learning new things all the time. My feeling is that the fishing is better from the shore than from a boat, if you can get to it. Sea trout seem to be spooky of boats, although not always. Easter is a good time, and you find some of the biggest sea trout coming in during April. As the summer kicks in, the average size goes down to around a pound to a pound and a quarter, with good fish of a pound and a half to two or so. Mind you, there's always the chance of big ones, but they tend to come to either bait anglers or spinners. For me, well, I personally always fish the fly.

"The sea trout are in the estuaries to feed, and feed hard. Their main target is the sand eel and, failing that, small fish of all types, so these are the food forms that you're imitating. It pays to experiment with various fly patterns, colours, and line densities. The Parson Tom works well and so do the Falkus Sunk Lure and the Gadget. I tend to fish these in traditional wet-fly techniques, but I'm always experimenting on rates of retrieve, depths, colours, and patterns.

LIVING AND LEARNING

"This is all about experimentation, and that's what makes it so exciting. For example, I'm nearly always fishing for the sea trout during the daytime, despite the old tradition that it was a waste of time going out until darkness had fallen. The state of the tide is another quandary, but I tend to like the hour before and the hour after the lowest tide. Certainly it's around this time that you'll see fish jumping everywhere, and that alone gives you a lot of confidence. Mind you, I must stress again that unpredictability is the name of the game. The more you fish a particular estuary – and there are sea trout up many of them – the more you learn which of the tides is likely to produce results. You get to know the bends, the bays, the different regimes of current flows, and just where fish like to feed and hang. You begin to realize how the wind affects everything, and which directions and strengths are good or bad. Light values come into it, too. It can fish well in bright conditions, and sometimes it's better when it's overcast. Dawn and dusk are interesting times."

I dropped Jim off at home to make tea for the kids and supper for the guests, and drove back north, to the quayside of Ballyshannon itself. It's a cracking fishery with huge atmosphere. Two guys were spinning for sea trout, with the type of half-heartedness that you associate with a blank day. No, they hadn't caught anything, but there had been fish jumping all the time. I saw them too – silver, darting shapes in the bottle-green water, slipping their way through the weed. Not big fish – the largest I saw was perhaps a shade over a pound and a half – but there were many, many of them. Just as appealing was the view out towards the sea, across the sandbanks and the dunes. You can see instantly why this type of fishing so appeals to a man like Jim Dillon, whose horizons extend so far. This is not the Drowse, with its manicured banks. This is the wild, demanding fishing on which a man like Dillon simply thrives.

MOORLAND PERFECTION *There's something about the small, wild browns from high altitude loughs that makes them uniquely special. Each and every water, no matter how small, seems to possess its own, recognizable fish patterns. The trout might not be large but they're wondrously shaped and coloured.*

THE OPEN SEA *There are many things compelling about the sea trout but one of their beauties is their nomadic behaviour, their gypsy-like lives, and the way they rejoice in the coming and going of the tide.*

DONEGAL EVENING *The rivers of Donegal are peaceful in a way that it's hard to imagine in this troubled 21st century. In the stillness of an autumn dusk, you can feel yourself transported to another time.*

An Excursion Into Donegal

Jim Dillon, knowing of my affection for small, spate salmon rivers, gave me a couple of last tips. He suggested that I carry on northwards, towards the town of Donegal, and then on into the county itself. He showed me the map and pointed out that if you look absolutely anywhere in Donegal, you'll see blue. The loughs tend to be small, but there are endless arteries of blue streams and rivers networking the entire area. There's more fishing up there than an angler could get to grips with in an entire lifetime, and Jim told me to visit at least a couple of the rivers.

My first destination was the waters that make up the Eanywater Fishery, not far from Donegal itself, out on the road west towards Killybegs. The fishery is part of a 50-square-mile catchment area made up of the Eany River, and the lower reaches of the Eanymore and the Eanybeg. A good deal of asking and exploring is called for, and on my visit there was precious little water or sign of fish moving. It is, however, a fabulous area, full of sights and sounds that had me entranced.

On to Owenea

I was tempted to stay longer, but I decided to push on into Donegal, to check out Jim's second tip, the Owenea River, close to Ardara at the head of the Loughros More Bay. The N56 is a stunning road as it heads north between the common and the Mulmosog mountains, taking you into country that becomes wilder and wilder. Ardara, however, was awash with festivities this particular Saturday night. The pubs along the high street were packed, the cafes and restaurants were doing a frantic business, and the crowd from a game of Gaelic football could plainly be heard in the still, evening air. I managed to beg a bed and breakfast, probably the last room in the town, and set out in the golden evening to look at the Owenea itself.

This is a gorgeous piece of water. I walked it for two, perhaps three, miles – a fraction of what is fishable. I saw salmon here and there, a couple of what I'm sure were sea trout, and good helpings of small, wild browns. What I didn't see was a single, solitary human being. Sure, the water was low and things could well have been different in a spate, but even so, this is fishing where sanity can prevail. This river is clearly well looked after, as the Fishery newsletter makes plain. The Fishery has put in 167 footbridges and walkways, five river bridges, 137 stepping stones and stiles, 17 signposts, two weirs, two reinforced areas of riverbank, and a disabled angling section along a length of beat three. It has also cared for the fish by imposing and policing rules – shrimp and prawn, for example, are banned, and fly fishing is hugely encouraged. There's been a lot of in-stream work as well, and the redd counts are encouraging. These stood at 205 in the winter of 1994/1995, but had risen to 694 by 1999/2000. It's a message that you cannot help but pick up from every Irish fishery: the Irish themselves deeply appreciate the wild fisheries that have been bestowed upon them, and are working tigerishly to protect and develop them. At their best, anglers are far more than simple sportsmen: they are true guardians of the stream.

The sun was almost down when I climbed to a hill and looked out due west over Loughros More Bay, into which the Owenea empties. The sea was a melting pot of gold poured between the velvet hues of Dawros Head and Loughros Point. I sat there until the sun was well down and the colours began to diminish.

OWENEA SUNSET *One of the glories of Irish fishing is the subtle light that comes into play both early and late in the day. The shadows, and the mists, and the shafts of gold and silver all make for a landscape touched with wonder.*

A MODEL FISHERY
The Lessons of Ballinlough

"Technology has helped all our protection services and, anyway, there's a spreading desire for change."

RAINBOW WARRIOR (opposite) *A lovely rainbow glides through the depths, ever on the lookout for food items. They may not be the wild, indigenous browns of Ireland but they're still sporting, and they do provide entertainment at times when the wild fish refuse to come out to play.*

THE BEAUTY OF BALLINLOUGH *You'd hardly believe this is a commercial fishery, so lost, lovely, and remote it is. If ever there were a model for other such places to follow, it is this enchanting piece of water.*

Once again, I owe all of the following to Ken Whelan. When we met on the Kerry Blackwater, I asked him about commercial trout fisheries in Ireland. Of course, there are some, especially closer to the cities, but Ken looked suitably blank. He mentioned one or two, but made it quite plain that Ireland has quite enough wild fishing, the sort of angling we all really want, for us not to bother too much with commercial alternatives. However, he did mention the exciting experiment of Ballinlough, and invited me out to his office at the Marine Institute Salmon Management Services Division in Newport if I should ever have a moment. How could I fail to find time for such an invitation?

We met up on a breezy day at his offices not far out of Newport, County Mayo, overlooking Clew Bay. As ever, Ken was in a bright, positive mood. "We're making great headway with the salmon stocks, there's no doubt. Technology has helped all our protection services and, anyway, there's a spreading desire for change. The ban on rod-caught salmon is excellent, and there's been a good response to the salmon-tagging system, which is leading to a much better overall understanding of populations. If you look at the drift-netting system, well, that's nearing its end anyway. The men doing it are pretty well at retirement age, and it's just going to peter out naturally, I guess. The anglers are showing good sense, and it's almost unknown

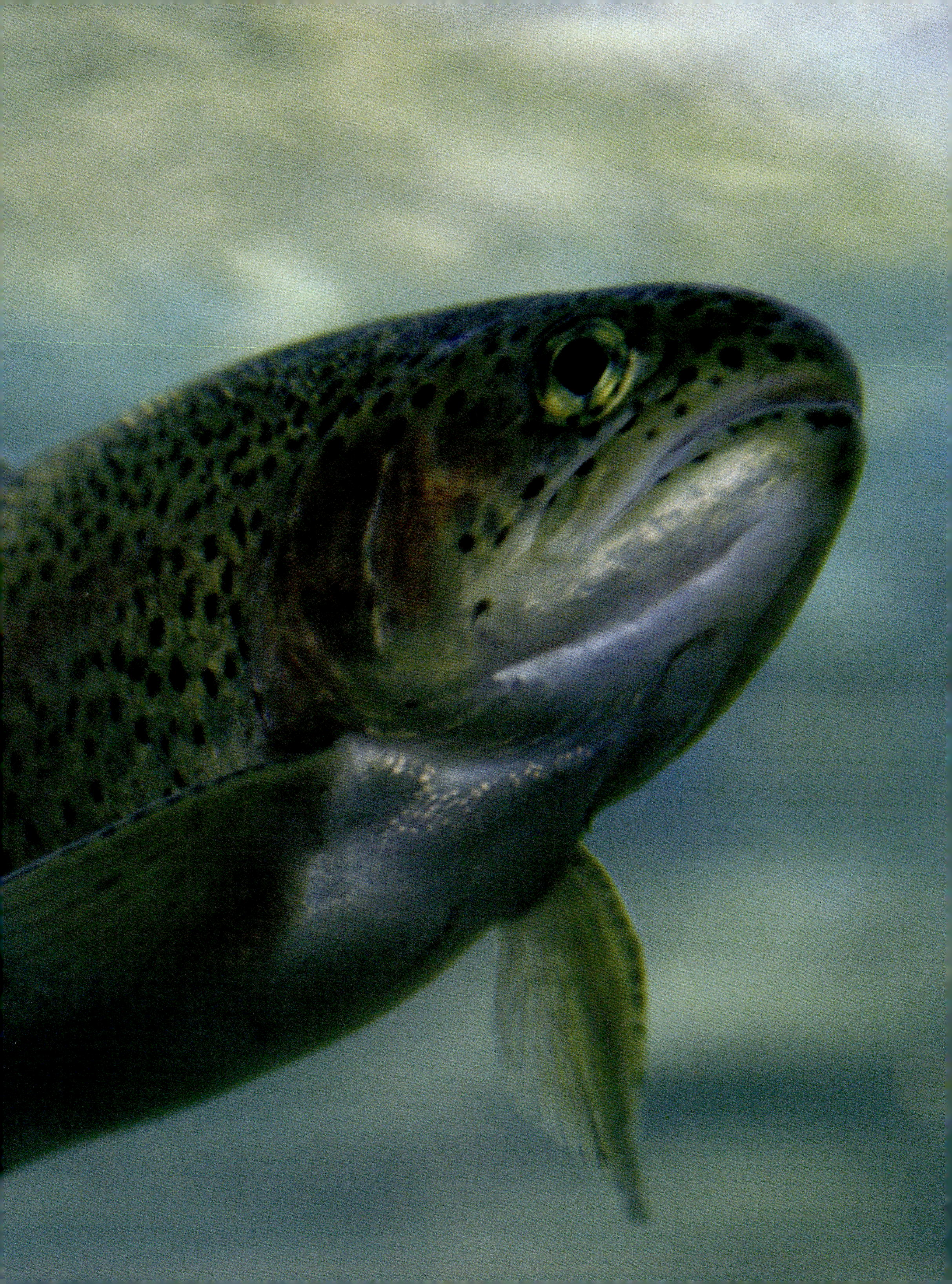

BEAUTY BEYOND COMPARE *There really were times when I simply had to pull the car over, get out, and just gaze at the wonder that was unfolding before me. Sometimes, like now, even taking a photograph spoiled the moment. Often it's enough to lock Paradise into your memory and not necessarily have it on celluloid.*

now to see a stale salmon lying on the grass. If we can convince everyone not to take four or six salmon in a day, then we will really be getting somewhere. Farmers are being forced to address the slurry and nitrate problems, and fish farmers around Waterville have shown that sea lice containment is possible."

IRELAND'S STRENGTHS

"We're also lucky that Irish rivers have such strong runs of grilse, and that we're not nearly as dependent on multi-winter sea fish as Scotland or, even more so, Norway. I was talking to the Fishery Officer on a lovely river up there where only 200 spawners return each year. They might average 30 pounds each and be whales of fish, but they don't represent a really sound fishing option. Give me Ireland, with its huge numbers of small fish. There's good private sector management throughout the country, too, providing good access for all. Prices can be kept down because there's plenty of competition and lots of good waters where anglers can go. What's more, the Irish are not just Catholic in religion but also in their fishing habits. There are 120,000 Irish fishermen, and they're willing to go for everything. For example, the trout anglers will have a bash for salmon or at sea fishing. The coarse and sea federations co-operate, and they can wield serious political clout." Ken is absolutely right, and it's a far cry from the situation in the UK, where there's such an enormous diversity of interests that any voice the anglers might have is split into innumerable babbling factions.

Taking Richie Johnston, one of my firmest Irish fishing pals, as an example, he seems to me to personify the very best of Irish angling. Richie is an expert on the midland loughs, but he regularly travels to Corrib, especially in the mayfly season. He'll also have a crack at sea fishing, and I first met him when he came over to England in pursuit of chub, carp, barbel, and roach. If that's not enough, his biggest speciality of all is pursuing Irish pike, and he's caught so many over 20 pounds that he can't remember them all.

"Yes, we have real diversity here," Ken continued. "One of my best day's sport was a couple of months ago, using a 9-weight fly rod, off a steep, rocky point cloaked in kelp, for pollock. I was using a fast-sinking line and fishing virtually vertically, drawing the fly up the face of the kelp. The pollock were darting out and grabbing the fly on its way to the surface, and the fight each time was breathtaking. Believe me, that day was one of the biggest thrills of my fishing life. You need florid fly designs – something like small pike flies that can get down really fast. These are superb locations, but they're not for the fainthearted. There's extremely deep water right under your feet, and the rocks can be like glass.

"It could well be that the Tourist Board needs to support a different mix of journalists if we're going to get this facet of Irish fishing across to the world. Perhaps, just perhaps, we've concentrated for too long on the standard fish and the well-known fisheries. There's so much out here that's exciting and different."

THE BALLINLOUGH EXPERIMENT

"Ballinlough is a perfect example of what can be done with good management policies. I first heard about the lough 20 years ago, when it was surrounded by fences and occasionally poached by the bad lads from Westport. There were rumours of some big fish, but nobody really knew much about it. Then, of course, the sea-trout fishing was really decimated and anybody with an interest in fisheries realized we had to do something. Ballinlough began to attract our attention more and more. Well, the story was that there were some big rainbows there, and a pal of mine, Mile Peters, proved the stories to be true with a brace of six-pounders in a single morning.

"Well, we closed Ballinlough for a year while we stocked it up and found funding for the road. The bulk of the stock were summerlings, going in at around six inches, although some were put in around double that size in October. Well, they grew on magnificently. We've had plenty of rainbows between 10 and 12 pounds, and we've experimented with char, triploids, and wild brown fry that have grown on to five- and six-pound fish. The lake is only around 15 feet deep, and very rich with wall-to-wall shrimp populations. Even surplus salmon smolts have gone in, and these have produced beautiful silver, one-pound salmon that have been responsible for rumours of silver rainbows! Most of these died off after a couple of years, but at least one lived on and was landed as a lovely six-pound grilse.

"Ballinlough is now run by the Northwest Fisheries Board, and although you might raise your eyebrows at some of the fish that have gone in there, it's all been done with careful thought and good scientific sense. I reckon it's a perfect example of how you can create a wonderful resource, and why not make things a bit of fun if you can? That's one of the problems of English fishing – just so many fisheries with the ubiquitous one-and-a-half-pound rainbow that everybody gets sick and tired of catching over and over again.

"There isn't much surface activity on Ballinlough, and that puts most people off using the dry fly. There is a modest hatch of spring olives, some buzzer activity, and some sedge, but never forget that the blind dry fly can be taken very well if just twitched to impart a little bit of life. At 55 acres, there's enough room on the lough for everybody, and it's in such a wondrous setting that it's really like being on a totally wild fishery. It's also kept crystal clear through the clever use of barley straw to combat algal blooms. The trick is knowing how much straw to put in – you've got to get the quantity to volume ratio spot on. The other point is to separate the straw, and not to leave it in bales. You also want it to be as wet as possible, because then it decomposes faster. What you do is make 20-foot-square corrals, put the bale in, but open it up and then separate all the straw. It also pays to turn the straw from time to time, for maximum efficiency. The straw obviously contains a natural algaecide, and if you use it properly as I've described, then you just don't get the bloom problem. The other bonus is that water shrimp absolutely love it, and you'll find boats glued to the corrals with anglers fishing shrimp patterns all around them."

On the way back south, I turned eastwards off the Westport road and down the track that leads to Ballinlough. Ken is absolutely right: this is a wonderful water. Two boats were out, and one angler was sitting in the fisherman's hut. Oh yes, he's had a great day and no mistake. It was his first trip, but he'd be coming again and again, for sure. Just three fish, but all fighting fit and in magnificent condition – a ferocious testament to the success of the whole venture.

LIQUID METAL *So rainbow trout aren't indigenous to Ireland, and so what? Fish like this are as beautiful as any brown trout or salmon. They're hard to catch and they're even harder to land. This is a sight at which no true angler can fail to marvel.*

THE MIDLAND LOUGHS
The Tale of Lough Sheelin

"... absolutely anything that Richie has to say about the state of Irish angling should be taken on board."

"There are so many pigs around Sheelin Lough that my dad says if you catch a trout you should eat it with apple sauce!" says Richie Johnston, the oldest and dearest of my Irish mates. Richie's dad, Des, is a devoted father, but his star act was to introduce Richie to fishing. The Johnstons are a fishing-crazed family: even his mother is at it, as obsessed as the men, and only stopping short of tying the legions of flies that come off the men's vices. Richie and Des have fished, together and separately, for decades, and absolutely anything that Richie has to say about the state of Irish angling should be taken on board.

Richie and I are standing beside Lough Sheelin, in the south of County Cavan, on a quiet autumn day. There's barely a ripple on the grey lough, and hardly a breath of breeze to stir the low cloud cover, and the sounds and the smells of Sheelin are starkly obvious to the senses. There's a heavy, porcine tang to the air, and I remark that I can hear pigs squealing. Richie laughs in a dry, dismissive sort of way.

"Oh, there are pigs all right, John, but you know the story. Agriculture still drives Ireland, and the number of pigs hereabouts was just allowed to get out of control. In the 1970s, Sheelin here was possibly the finest wild brown trout water in Europe, and then we caught pig mania. So many pigs produced so much slurry, it made no difference whether it was poured into pits or onto the land – come the rain that we have over here in Ireland, it ended up in the rivers or the lough. And what happened? Well, Sheelin lost its clarity and its purity, and turned from a trout water to a roach and rudd lake. When the wild browns went to spawn, they found the gravels buried under slurry. It's one of the saddest examples of how greed can ruin the countryside."

THE FLEET (opposite) *You don't find more beautiful boats anywhere in the world than you do in Ireland. It's as though the ghillies themselves appreciate how fine a boat can look and how this grace can enhance the whole day afloat.*

MAN WITH A MISSION *Richie Johnston, as good a friend as a man can ever have, punches a line out over Lough Sheelin. It's not what it was? Well perhaps not, but even in its decline Richie has managed nine-pound wild browns from this magical water.*

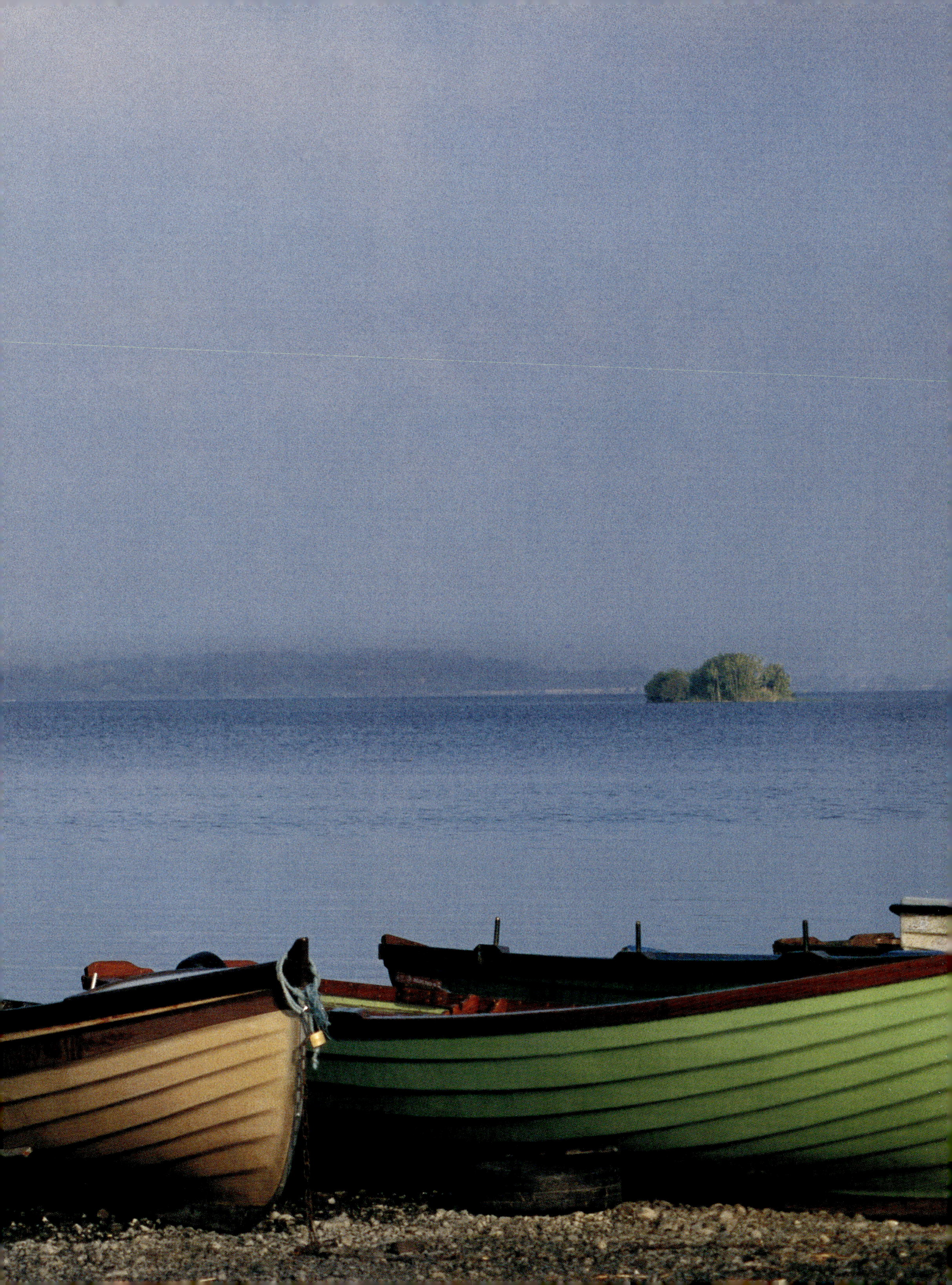

SWAN LAKE *Okay, your average picnicker or walker can appreciate sights such as this, a group of swans out on Lough Owel, but it's the angler who has learnt to live with such beauty and truly appreciate the waters of Ireland for what they are.*

In the stillness, we can hear, as well as see, fry scattering some 30 yards out. Trout, perhaps, but from the splashiness of the swirls, the culprits could easily be perch, Richie speculates. Sheelin is now just full of fish, and to prove this, Richie flicks out a pike fly on a nine-weight, the only gear he has with him. On the second pull he's into a fish, which somersaults free. "Thank God for that. Just a bloody stocky. I'm sure you recognized the horrid, squat little thing," he snorts – and he packs up on the spot.

"It's not that I've got anything against pigs personally," Richie says when we're back in the bar of the hotel, overlooking the water. "That's why I'm tucking into a ham sandwich now! It's only farming practices that have made them the menace they are. And malpractices, too, come to that. You wouldn't believe the corruption and rule bending that has gone on over the years to get more pig units up and running. There's no more classic case in the whole of Ireland of how to muck up the environment."

A Catalogue of Factors

However, this isn't the whole story, not by a long chalk. Once Sheelin began to lose its pre-eminence as a wild brown trout fishery, then other factors started to kick in. "Many people don't think the Fisheries Board has helped in the way it should have done," Richie says thoughtfully, considering another round of ham sandwiches.

"Rather than getting to the root of the problem and trying to reinstate the lough, they've taken the easy way out, and that's by stocking it massively with farmed browns. I don't blame them in one way: all these midland loughs are important both for tourism and for the Dublin angling population, and they've got to have something to fly fish for. If the browns aren't holding up, then the Fisheries people thought to give us all farmed browns. You can see the logic of it. On the one hand, anglers, some of them quite inexpert, can come from Dublin just an hour away and catch five or six fish in a day. It gives them pleasure and it brings in revenue, and it might inspire them to take up wild trout fishing in the future. All that's good – if you overlook just how miserable the farmed browns are to catch, and how easy, come to that. On the other hand, while a good number of people are happy, the real problem is ignored and there's little incentive to set about proper, but unpopular, solutions. There are other crackpot elements, too. For example, the Fisheries Board tries to remove as many pike as possible and that just leads to a proliferation of roach, rudd, and jacks. They won't let you dead bait for pike either, in case you catch the odd big brown that's left, and they won't let you pike fish in the winter, which makes no sense at all!"

"... while a good number of people are happy, the real problem is ignored..."

LOOKING ON THE BRIGHT SIDE

"There are still some positive things to be said about Sheelin. There are still some wild browns left in the lough, and it's only a few years ago – well, 1991 to be exact – that I had my own biggest brown from the place, a near 10-pounder taken on a dapped Daddy, proving that the wild fish have always kept a toehold here. There's a small head of very large browns left, and to some degree they've profited from the explosion of cyprinids. Nowadays, there are huge amounts of fry for them to gorge upon from the late summer onwards. For me, I'd much, much rather the stocked browns were kept out of the place, to give you more of a chance of stalking what browns are left. Of course, this is very difficult fishing indeed, and not for the likes of many, but I'd personally have one special fish in five outings than five mediocre fish each outing. No, stocked fish are not the answer. They've got no fins, no tails, and they're bred like battery hens. Stockies are just a quick fix, and nothing more than that.

"The people that really are doing something about Sheelin are the members of the Lough Sheelin Trout Preservation Association. These guys have done wonders to right the wrongs that have been heaped on the lough. They've made Herculean attempts to clean up the feeder streams and make them attractive again to spawning wild browns. They've also introduced fingerling browns into the streams, so they can leech back into the lough to kick-start a revival. This is a really serious conservation force that's done wonders to raise money, raise awareness, and preserve the wild brown. The trouble is that for every spawning stream they save, another pig unit is built and another belt of rain washes the slurry into the system again. It's heartbreaking. Sometimes it feels like one step forward and two miserable steps backward."

EVENING BLISS We're just an hour out of Dublin, among the Midland Loughs at sunset. The lone angler may be a dentist, or a lawyer, or a road worker. It doesn't matter. The man's labours for the day are over and now his heart is given over to gladness.

STEELY SHEELIN *Forget the pigs, and forget the damage that's been done. Sheelin is still a lake of magic and mystery and given the enormous amount of good will felt towards it, it is almost bound to become a fabulous fishery again soon.*

AND AS FOR THE FUTURE?

"Well, things have to get better, and there's certainly more awareness now. Tourism is important, and people certainly don't come over here for the weather. If we're going to keep on attracting international anglers, then we've got to give them a worthwhile experience, and that means wild fish – not blasted stockies all the time. The LSTPA have laid down the blueprint, and now it's time for serious government money to take up the challenge. If more money is needed to help the wild brown situation, then why not promote fishing for the bream, perch, tench, roach, and rudd?

"The other good news around here is Lough Ennell. This remains very clear and very rich, with serious duck fly and mayfly hatches. The sedge hatch is also prolific, and there are vast amounts of snails, shrimps, and fry. It's a great lough, with some fantastic fish, but the clarity and the wealth of food do make for difficult fishing.

"Owel is an important water as well, but it doesn't have quite the number of spawning streams that Ennell does. Although it has good wild fish populations, these are supplemented a good deal by stocked fish – and you know what I think to those! You shouldn't forget the smaller loughs either – Lene, Glore, Bane, and Derravaragh. These are important wild trout loughs, too, and they're well looked after. The 'Lough Bane Anglers' was formed about 12 years ago, and they're doing an excellent job. For every greedy angler who's just out to fill a plastic bag, there's a caring, conservation-minded fisherman who returns his fish and works hard to improve the waters. The tide is turning, and that's another reason for thinking the future's bright here."

RICHIE JOHNSTON'S MIDLAND TROUT TIPS

The season on Sheelin, Ennell, and Owel kicks off on March 1st, but the fishing tends to be very bleak and few locals can be seen out. On Sheelin, the generally held beginning of everything is, appropriately, St Patrick's Day.

Most locals use intermediate and sinking lines early on. Wet flies and nymphs seem to do the trick, and Minkies are proving ever more popular. At first local anglers laughed at these, but no longer! In the early part of the season it is mostly stockies that are caught, and the wild browns are rare.

There are big hatches of duck fly in April on Sheelin, Ennell, and Owel. Floating lines, allied with standard duck fly patterns and especially epoxy buzzers work well. Mostly, the technique is to fish from drifting boats using drogues, if necessary, to slow them down. Anchoring up is very rare. It's important at this point of the year to keep de-greasing the leader to make sure the flies work beneath the surface film.

By May, the olives are showing. This is all floating-line work using standard wet flies, and dries during hatches. The various Klinkhammer patterns are proving very popular (and they're also well worth trying on the western loughs).

The mayfly season is good on Sheelin and Ennell, but the hatches are sparse on Owel. Favourite flies are various Wulffs, especially royal and green. On Ennell, the spent gnat fishing can be excellent, but you need consistently warm evenings and then sport is often just for a handful of nights. On Sheelin, mayflies hatch right into late June and even early July, although not in the earlier vast numbers.

Just after the mayfly hatches, look out for the Welshman's button appearing – a sedge with an easily distinguishable yellow body. By July, most of the fish are on fry and, although you can catch them on fry imitations, fishing in this month is generally considered poor.

During August and September, the locals are out dapping, mostly with naturals. This is how I caught my own nine-pound thirteen-ounce fish. Favourites are grasshopper, Daddies, and crickets. What you need is a good south or southwesterly wind, and fish both the shallows and the deep.

Crickets are really proving popular at the moment. Go into any pet shop in Mullingar or Dublin and ask for crickets, and they'll know exactly what you want them for… and it won't be for your pet snake! This easy option will save you time tramping the fields looking for grasshoppers. They're hardy and they stay on the hook for ages.

By late September, most of the trout migrate into the river mouths waiting for rain and their spawning runs upstream. The fish now are full of roe, and all should go back.

It's traditional that on the last day of the season there is a major competition on Sheelin. This is really just an excuse for parties and barbecues and, today, all fish are uniformly returned – hopefully a sign of our much more caring times.

A LOVELY FISH *A trout recuperates in the margins before it is released and returned to fight another day.*

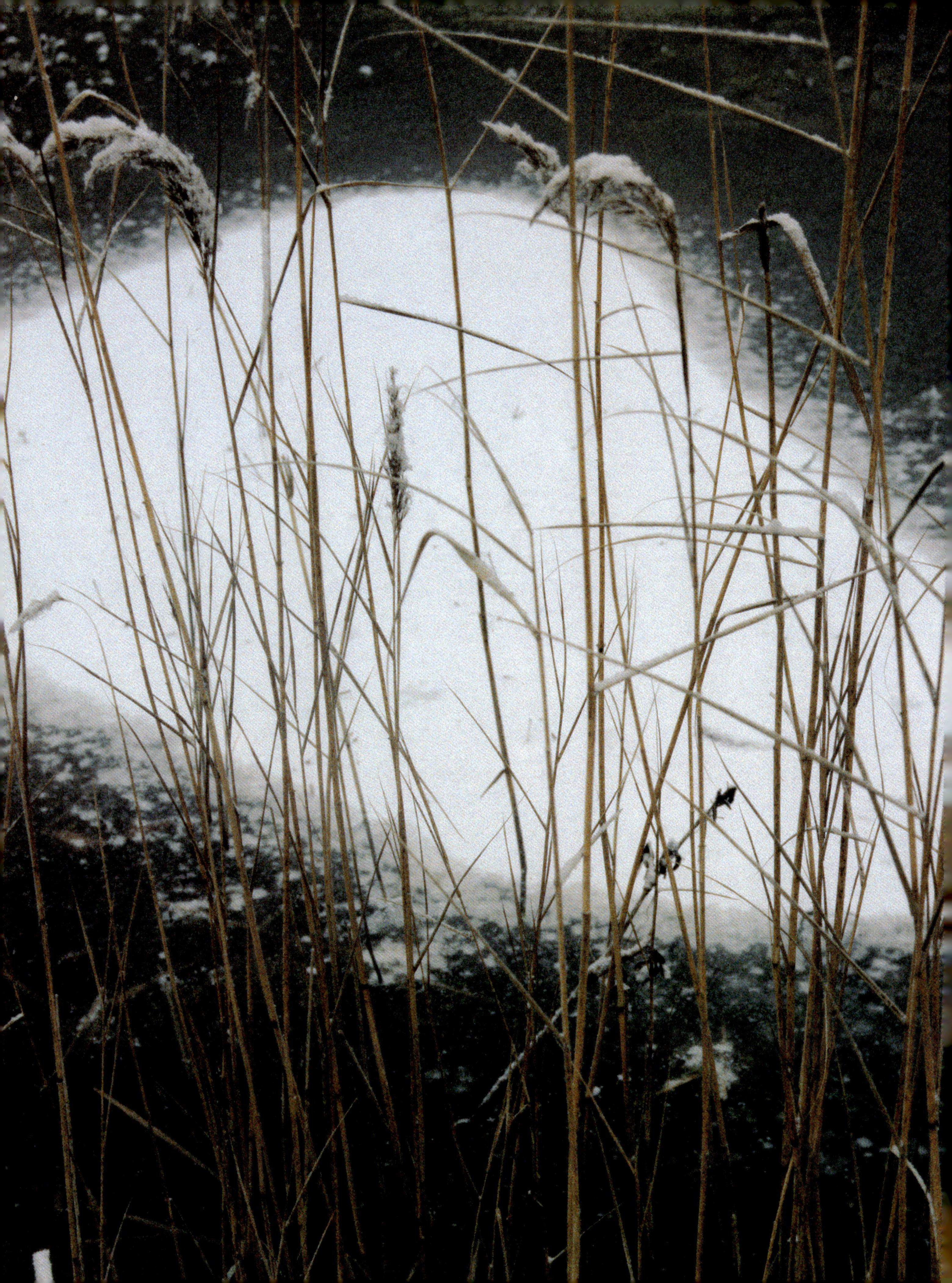

Winter

"Suddenly, in that wintry twilight, I was made aware of the Partry Mountains and the incredible beauty of the place I'd been fishing."

My first and most dramatic experience of Ireland's winter weather took place many, many years ago when my dear friend Fred Buller lent me his cottage just outside Ballinrobe, on the shores of Lough Mask. My plan was to fish for pike and, on the opening of the trout season, to combine that attack with the pursuit of ferox trout.

But plans in Ireland in the winter can frequently go awry, and week upon week – yes, I'm talking a whole five weeks – was spent in the teeth of an almost unceasing storm. Night after night, the walls of Fred's ancient cottage shook and trembled before the gales. The windows were lashed with rain and sleet virtually every hour out of the twenty-four. I couldn't get dry. I couldn't get warm. I ransacked Fred's supply of peat and had electric heaters running high, but still I shivered and shook all through those miserable, bone-aching days.

There were the odd times when I managed to get out on the lough, but to do so I really did risk life and limb. The winds were unrelenting and this was my first visit to mighty Mask, with its rocks and reefs. Add to that the unreliability of the engine of my boat in those days – the aptly named *Black Pig* – and there were times when I felt lucky to return to Cuslough in one piece! My diary of those weeks makes gruesome reading, and I certainly wouldn't consider now what I took in my stride then...

"3.35 p.m. and I have had to stop trolling, pull off the arm of Mask, and sit the day away in a backwater. The wind is now gusting at least force 8, and a farmer even called to me a few minutes ago to come in. 'Storms, terrible storms,' he shouted. 'Give it up boy, now, when you've got a chance.'"

In truth, most of the days were spent huddled in the bars of the town, sampling the Guinness from half a hundred pumps! During that winter month, more than at any other time, I learnt to appreciate the wit and the generosity of the Irish people. I believe they really felt for me, shared my disappointment, and prayed with a fervour equal to mine that the weather gods would soon be kind. The prayers went largely unheeded, but there was one late afternoon...

The day had been exceptionally stormy, and I hadn't even considered taking the boat from the security of the bay. At around four o'clock, as the light was going, I was on the point of giving up on yet another futile day when, quite suddenly, the wind dropped completely and the cloud began to lift. I watched it rise like a veil being lifted from the face of a bride, and what a face was revealed. In all those storm-thrashed weeks I'd never realized there were mountains to the west of Lough Mask! Suddenly, in that wintry twilight, I was made aware of the Partry Mountains and the incredible beauty of the place I'd been fishing. It felt like a dream, but I knew that it was real enough. All the suffering had suddenly become worthwhile. If ever I knew I was going to love Ireland until my dying day, it was in that awe-filled moment. And, yes, I even caught a pike!

WINTER ON THE WATER
Time for Reflection

"... no matter how much the wind howls, the sleet rakes down, and spring seems an eternity away, you can still keep in touch."

It is now wintertime, and between October and March very few flies indeed are cast in Ireland. The country lacks the grayling rivers that keep the die-hard enthusiast involved throughout the winter in the UK, even though, on my travels, I've found dozens of streams that I'm sure would prove welcoming homes for grayling. However, no matter how much the wind howls, the sleet rakes down, and spring seems an eternity away, you can still keep in touch. Fly tying is a source of succour for many, and now is the time to boost your stocks of Green Peters, Bumbles of all colours, Bibios, and scores of different shrimp patterns for your days on the Moy, the Blackwater, or the Drowse. Always tie at least three or four of each fly in any particular colour on any given size of hook. There is nothing more infuriating than finding the taking fly on a particular day only to lose it and discover you don't have a substitute. It's almost better not to unpick the lock in the first place.

Or you can read about fishing, tucked up by a fire or woodburner, a malt whisky to hand. Angling literature throughout the world is richer than you'll find in any other sport, and particularly so about Ireland. Perhaps you can locate some of the older books. *An Angler's Paradise* by F. D. Barker, first published in 1929, is perhaps my own personal favourite. Fortunately, it was reprinted by The Fly Fisher's Classic Library a few years ago, so copies can still be found. If you want an image of an Irish paradise, then you just can't do any better. Grimble is made of stern, gristly stuff, but

A TIME FOR ROACH (opposite) *Conditions like these are a roach man's delight – a quiet, mild day in winter, and the river oozes through its bends where roach play and feed in the deep, slow water.*

SHAFTS OF GOLD *Ireland never looks better than it does in the winter, at sunset when the trees are stark and bare but the sky is still full of light and promise.*

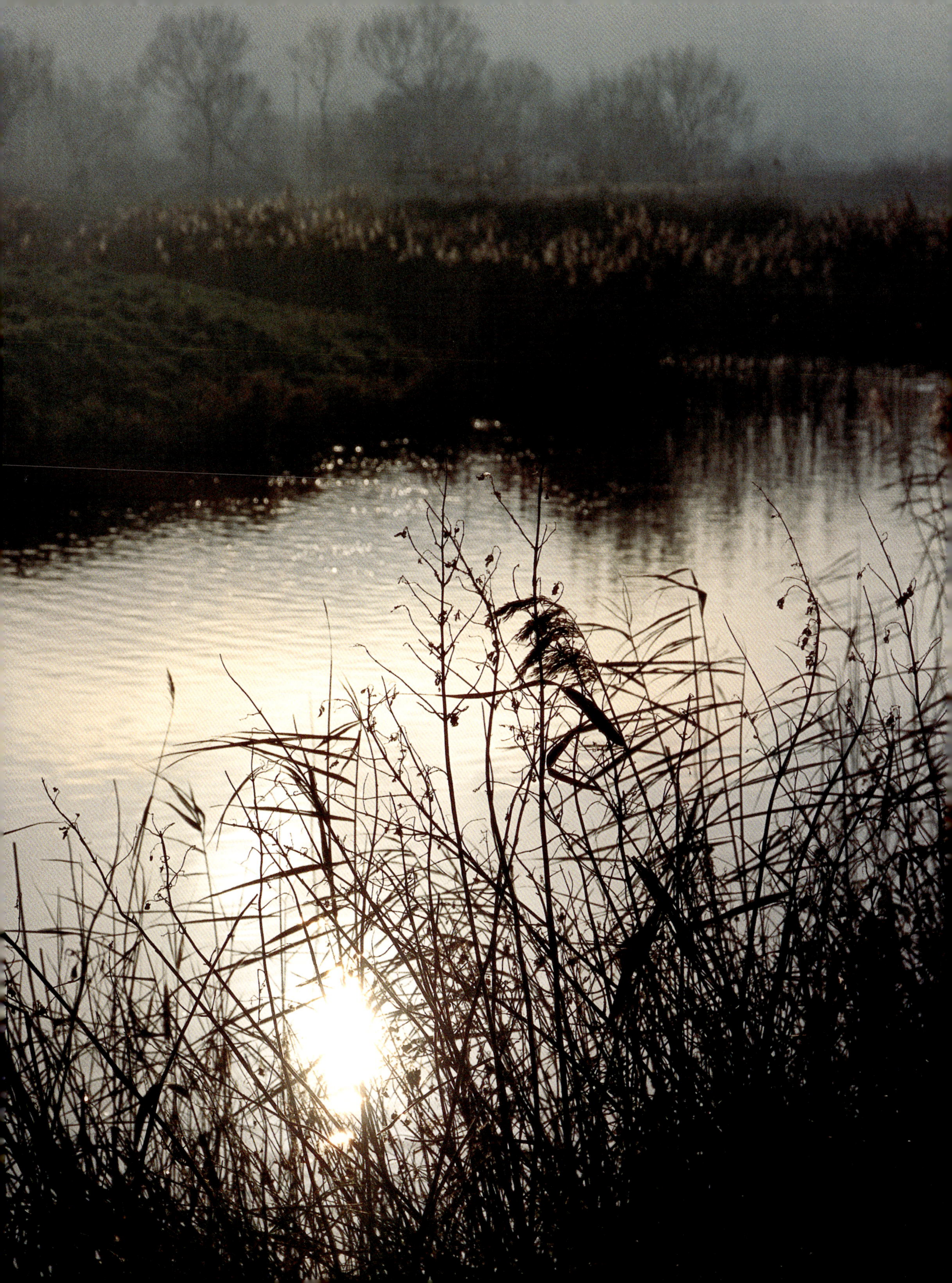

BENEATH THE ICE *Even though the weather is cold and the lake is sheathed in ice, this pike is still on the fin, prowling, looking for food, and capable of providing good sport.*

PIKE MAN'S DAWN *A cauldron of mist, the lake lies brooding and expectant. It's now, before the sun comes up and the air glows bright, that the pike angler has the best chance of success.*

I adore *The Angler's Guide to the Irish Fisheries* by Joseph Adams, first published in 1924. The photographs are magical and they show scenes that are frequently little changed. The writing is gushy, but it's fun, and Adam's enthusiasm will make you twitch and stir in the cosiest of armchairs. *A Game Fisher in Ireland* by Colin McKelvie, published in 1989 by the Ashford Press, is enormously erudite and interesting. Colin himself is a jewel of a man, and his wit and knowledge glitter throughout the book. And, of course, if you haven't got a Peter O'Reilly volume to hand, then you just cannot be serious about your Irish fly fishing.

IN COUNTY MAYO

How will the long, dark winter months be spent by our friends over there in Ireland itself? Well, Graham Williams doesn't have a bad time of it down in Pontoon, on the shores of Conn and Cullin. "Winter in Pontoon is when anglers and boatmen alike pay the price for the glories of the summer. Once we've hauled the boats in and cleaned them, we wait for the inevitable rain and gales that are all part of winter over here. The catchment area for Conn and Cullin is absolutely massive, and it's not unusual to see the lakes rise three feet in as many days. That extra yard of water on top of 27 square miles of lough is like emptying the whole of Cullin into Conn!

"There are all sorts of winter chores to be done, and it's not just sorting out the boats and engines that demands our attention. Now is the time to clean lines and check backing. Reels can be stripped down, cleaned, and oiled. Rods should be checked out and dodgy eyes replaced, and make sure you store everything in dry, reasonably warm places where the mice can't nibble at the rod butts. Check all your bags and jackets, too, and throw out the festering bag of worms that you'd forgotten.

"Flies are the tools of our trade, so those we've managed to keep our hands upon throughout the season are now sorted, sharpened, and generally made shipshape. But our artificials fly away faster then swallows throughout the season, and it's the winter months that give us the time to replenish all our stocks. I always say that those of us who have taken the opportunity are easily spotted – we're completely myopic, with a range of vision down to six inches. By January, we're bumping into bar stools and picking up other people's drinks... well, I assume this is down to the fly tying.

"The bar is important to us here in Pontoon – it's the hub of our world, the place where we can take time to remember the last season and dream of the next. It's good when the gales roar, the walls shake, and the sleet slashes its way across Cullin and batters the windows. As we say, 'It's a day for the high stool and the top shelf.'

"But there are mild, quiet, and calm days, too, and periods of high pressure with blue skies and sharp night frosts when we can still enjoy our sport. The pike fishing is excellent on Lough Levalley and Lough Derryhick both, and a day's walking and spinning soon passes and makes you believe you've earned that high stool! And if I reach for my gun, the dog's over the moon. He knows he's got a day walking up for pheasant, snipe, and woodcock, and we'll come home exhausted, wet through, and ready to dine on a meal to die for. No. Winter I can live with, make no mistake."

IN COUNTY SLIGO

It's much the same at Arrow Lodge with Rob and Stephanie. "By mid-November the lodge is quiet and the very last of the fishermen have gone. Like guides all over Ireland, we lay up our boats, sand them down, and give them a coat of varnish. Engines, too, have to be looked after and then, like as not, we'll go away for a few weeks and enjoy a real break, preferably in the sun, because we'll see precious little of that in January and February. These can be killer months. At times the weather just seems to get worse and worse, and you think that the rain and the winds will never abate. But there are good days interspersed with the bad and, suddenly, you see the incredible beauty of Arrow again – the alder trees purple with buds, the reeds bleached fawn and set against the gunmetal of Lough Arrow under the lowering winter skies, the reds of the dogwood and the wildfowl honking in as the dusk slips in early. At this time of the year, the sun also sets straight in front of us, right down the lake, so we catch the last vestiges of light. There are so many wildfowl that we're both now avid birdwatchers... it really is like living next to the most fabulous of reserves."

"Now is the time to clean lines and check backing. Reels can be stripped down, cleaned, and oiled. Rods should be checked out and dodgy eyes replaced."

THE CORRIB BOATS *These sleek vessels don't remain beautiful by themselves. Winter is the time to work on them, repair the wear and tear, and restore them to their full glory.*

PIKE ON THE FLY *This pike, weighing about 12 or 15 pounds, I suppose, has taxed my tackle and my fishing ability to the limit. We love our trout, we adore our salmon, but let's not neglect the humble pike.*

"It's an awesome spectacle, and a reminder that spring is on its way and that snowdrops are probably on the ground."

IN COUNTY FERMANAGH

For Richie Johnston, the winter windows of reasonable weather glitter bright. He can ignore his trout fishing with a clear conscience and set about the fish that I believe are, deep down, his truest love. Now he can really investigate the scores of pike waters that he hears about through his trouting summer. We can envy him his remote waters with pike of livid, flaring colours, and that dagger-thrust of anticipation when a lure is taken or a dead bait is snaffled. That's the beauty of pike fishing on waters like these – you just don't know. That bend in your rod could signal a four-pound jack or a 40-pound monster on her way to the spawning beds. It was Richie who alerted me to one of my most cherished Irish piking venues – Belle Isle Estate, on the northern tip of Upper Lough Erne. The castle is ancient, the estate, spread over eight picturesque islands, is vast, and it offers some of the most untapped pike fishing in Europe. Here there is a maze of waterways – tiny channels, lagoons, rivers, and the open lough itself. There are fish everywhere but, even after constant visits, location is still a huge problem. There's just so much water and so many possibilities, like Ireland itself.

There's one particular bay right in front of the castle that I long to fly fish through February and March, perhaps into April, depending upon climatic conditions, and that brings us to another absorbing question. What are the fish doing throughout the winter when we have left them to their own devices? The pike, certainly, will be sniffing out the drains, the dykes, the ditches, and all the shallow, weeded water they can find to lay their eggs. The smaller males might well go into these bays and backwaters first, while the big females patrol the drop-offs, moving slowly, conserving their energy, but still with an eye open for an easy meal. Then, when the water temperatures approach the critical point for them, they'll move slowly, stealthily, throughout the long night into water often no deeper than their backs to begin spawning. The males will weigh between five and ten pounds, and the females can be anything up to six times that weight. It's an awesome spectacle, and a reminder that spring is on its way and that snowdrops are probably on the ground.

In the latter days of the winter, you might well imagine Bob, one of the leading guides at the Blackwater Lodge, huddled into the dead reeds, fishing for roach. "At this time of the year, when the nights begin to draw out, the roach assemble in vast numbers. If you really know the river, you can pinpoint the deep bends where they will be holed up for weeks before moving away to shallower waters to spawn. Perhaps it's the cold that drives them down into the deep, slow holes. Maybe they save their energy there, out of the current. Perhaps food stocks attract them, or it could be that shoaling up like this helps protect them from predators. A mild, grey afternoon, teetering towards dusk, and a little red float inching its way down with the lazy current. Again and again it disappears. A bent rod and a glimpse of the pearly scales set against the steely water. They're not salmon, true, nor trout, but they're perfect fish in their own way, and they really light up the last days of winter."

SPAWNING TIME

So how do the salmon and trout spend the dark months? Graham watches the battle of the species on the feeder streams of Conn and Cullin. "Sadly, as with any mixed trout and salmon lough, there is a tussle here for survival. The trout spawn some time in October and, come December, just as their eggs are maturing, the salmon move onto the same redds. So much of that trout spawn is going to be laid to waste as the salmon scoop deeper into the gravel to cut out their own redds. Oh yes, man may be a cruel creature all right, but maybe he learnt that from watching nature too closely."

Mind you, man isn't all bad. Think of Peter Mantle and his companions at the Delphi fishery tagging those tens of thousands of smolts during the coldest days of January, all to put right a system vandalized by commerce. Here's Rob again from Arrow Lodge. "The lough is fed by several small feeder streams that are mainly spring fed. The trout spawn in these comparative dribbles of water, one of which is the boundary of our land. The Fisheries monitor these streams very closely indeed. 'Ours', if you can call it that, is called the Derry Lea, and this year I'll be able to go out on spawning patrol every night. Yes, it can be a spooky, cold, rainy, and windswept experience, but the sights that you see in your torch beam are extraordinary."

And what of the salmon themselves, arguably the star of the Irish scene these days? They are spawning everywhere at the rump of the year as the fish flock to their

PIKER'S SUNSET *The day is almost over and the light is fading, but you can be fairly sure that there will still be a fish on the prowl. Just give it that last half an hour and you could be amply rewarded.*

spawning grounds. Rob, again, describes the route of his own local salmon. "You'll remember the salmon in the Ballysadare River that I introduced you to. Well, this is their moment. The River Ballysadare is formed by the Unshin, draining Lough Arrow, and the Owenmore, which drains Templehouse Lake. Those salmon that make it up the waterfalls of the Ballysadare hook a ride up the Owenmore and follow the meanders for about nine miles as far as Templehouse Lake. This is fed by the Owenbeg that flows in about half way up, so that's another four or five miles those salmon move. They follow the Owenbeg system, which after three miles becomes known as the Owenboy River, and you'll see this sources a further 10 miles away in the Ox Mountains, and this is where the salmon finally choose to spawn.

"If you take the trouble and the time to find the salmon at this moment, believe me, it's a sight worth seeing. The females do the work, canting onto their flanks to use their tails to the best advantage. Their bodies flex in dynamic bursts of activity and the gravels are sheared. This, of course, is known as the cutting of the redds. The force of water produced by the body and pounding tail are sufficient to move even quite large stones downriver. These, along with gravel and sand, form piles of loose spoil at the tail of the depression. All this takes hours, but there are periods of rest in between. In the end, you'll have a trough a few inches deep and about as long as the female salmon herself. The male attends, sometimes quite passively, but very frequently chasing away competitors, trout, and even precocious male salmon parr that are trying to get in on the spawning act themselves. The dominant male will establish himself, and his hook jaw with its savagely sharp teeth can quite easily inflict mortal wounds on smaller rivals. This is his moment. It's what he's lived his life for, and he's not going to let it slip away from him.

"If you take the trouble and the time to find the salmon at this moment, believe me, it's a sight worth seeing."

THE LAST RUN HOME *The salmon are ghosting now to their spawning beds, to their final resting places. Spawning will be tumultuous. Their racked bodies will have no more strength left in them. This is both an ending and a new beginning.*

"At last, when satisfied that the nest is ready, the hen fish presses her abdomen hard down into the redd that she has made. Instinctively, the male fish draws close alongside and just a little forward of her, and starts to quiver violently. This is the stimulus for the hen fish to shed her eggs. The mouths of both salmon gape wide open as they reach climax. The stream of pale orange spawn extrudes from her vent, mixing instantly with the milky cloud of silt that spurts simultaneously from his.

"Spent and disorientated, his life's work now completed, the male fish drifts off a few yards downstream. His mate, meanwhile, always has one last task to fulfil. Just a little upstream of the nest, the exhausted hen fish repeats the same tail-flapping exercise that she used to cut the redd initially. This time her purpose is to cover the precious fertilized eggs and to bury them under a protective layer of gravel and small stones. Huge numbers of eggs can be shed and fertilized – an average female lays some 5,000 eggs. They will remain here all winter, lying among the pebbles in which they've been buried. In this wild, lonely place, at this desolate time of the year, it's a sight that you will never forget, John."

Most of the adult salmon now drift away to die, but their usefulness to the river system is not yet done. At this cruel time of the year, their bodies provide food for predators both in and out of the water. When the herons, otters, stoats, and owls have all taken their fill, the carcass and all its nutrients will dissolve back and be recycled into the stream in which it died.

DEATH IN WINTER *A spent salmon lies dead on the ice flows. Its task of renewal is done. Its destiny has been fulfilled.*

THE MARCH SUNSHINE *The angler's year is starting all over again. March is making its entrance. Soon the duck fly will be up, and then the mayfly. There's always another season, always another day. There will always be the finest of all fishing in Ireland.*

Index

A
Adams, Joseph 65, 88
agricultural pollution 142–4
Allen Ward, Jon 128
Ally's Shrimp 35
An Angler's Paradise,
  F.D. Barker 151
The Angler in Ireland,
  Ken Whelan 83
*The Angler's Guide to the
  Irish Fisheries*, Joseph
  Adams 151
Ardara 134–5
Arrow Lodge 20, 108, 153, 155
Arrow, Lough 20–27, 108, 111–12, 153
  fishing methods 26–7
Ashford Castle 12–19

B
Ballina 118–19
Ballinlough 136–41
Ballynahinch Castle 36–43
  fishing methods 42
Ballysadare River 114–15, 156
Ballyshannon 132, 133
Belle Isle Estate 154
Bibio 131
big fish, playing 70–71
Black Gnat 125
Black Goldfinch 71
Black Pennell 31, 35, 42, 43
Blackwater Lodge 56–60, 154
Blackwater, River, Co Cork 56–60, 102
Blackwater, River, Co Kerry 80
boat fishing 19
bonefish 24, 104
brickeen 16
Bricklieve Mountains 20
Bridgetown Priory 59, 60
brown trout 22, 33, 69, 100, 101, 146
Bundoran 132
Bundorragha, River 88–93
Butcher 43
Butler Arms Hotel 74
buzzer 18, 20

C
caddis larva 18
Caragh, Lough 44–5
Caragh, River 46–7
Carra, Lough 101
Castleconnell 64–6
  fishing methods 66, 71
Chaplin, Charlie 72
char 33
Clan Chief 131
Claret Bumble 26, 35
Claret Hopper 131
Cloon, Lough 44–5
Collie Dog 35
Conn, Lough 120–27, 152, 154
Conneely, Mike 36, 39
Connemara Black 26, 42
Cooper, Joshua 114
Corrib, Lough 12–19, 96
  fishing methods 17, 18
Costello, Frank 13, 17–19
Crichton, Captain 25
crickets 147
Cullin, Lough 120–27, 152, 154
Cummings, Frank 38–9
Currane, Lough 72–9

D
dace 102
Daddy Longlegs 35, 107, 147
daphnia feeders 99
dapping 52, 147
Dawros Head 135
Delphi Fishery 88–93, 155
Derravaragh, Lough 146
Derryhick, Lough 153
Dever, John 125–6
Devon Minnow 50
Dillon, Jim 128–34
Doherty, Mick 67–9
Dooras Peninsula 99
Drowse, River 130, 132
duck fly 18, 20, 99, 146, 147

E
Eany, River 134
Eanywater Fishery 134
Ennell, Lough 146
Erne, Lough 128, 132–3, 154
Erne, River 128
  fishing methods 132–3

F
Factor, Kevin 49
Falkus Sunk Lure 132
Farlow, fishing tackle 25
ferox trout 16, 17–18, 33, 100
fish farms, effects of 33, 39, 90
float tubing 108–13
Flying C 50
Folan, Colin 31–5
Foy, Jimmy 12–16

G
Gadget 132
Galway 116–18
A Game Fisher in Ireland,
  Colin McKelvie 151
Garry Dog 71
gillaroo 131
Glencar 44–51
  fishing methods 50–51
Glore, Lough 146
Golden Olive Bumble 131
goldhead nymph 69
grasshopper 147
Grasshopper Cottage 99
Green Dabbler 35
Green Peter 27, 35
Guering, Patrick 67

HIJ
Hairy Mary 71
Hardy, fishing tackle 25
Hare's Ear 69
Healy's Hotel 120–27
Heath, Gordon 120
Hollow Stoat 59
Inagh, Lough 28
  fishing methods 35
John Anthony shrimp 119
Johnston, Richie 139, 142, 154

K
Keane, Ted 56
Keays, Richard 8, 62–7
  Eleanor 62–4
Kenmare, River 80
Kerry 72–9, 80–87
Killybegs 134
Klinkhammer 31, 147

L
Lemon and Grey 50
Leonard, fishing tackle 25
Limerick 62–71

Lough Inagh Lodge 28–35
Loughros More Bay 134–5
Lough Sheelin Trout Preservation Assoc. 145

MN

mackerel 34, 104–5
Maharaja Jam Sahib of Nawangar 36–8
Maloney, Rob 20–24, 108–12, 153, 156–7
  Stephanie 22, 24–5, 153
Mantle, Peter 90–91, 155
Mask, Lough 101
Maumturk Mountains 12
mayfly 18, 27, 33, 99, 119, 125, 146, 147
  dapping 52, 147
  lifecycle 53
Melvin, Lough 128–32
Melvin, River 128
Michelangelo 71
Millbank House 62–4
Minky 16
minnow 16
Moy, River 118–19
Mulcair, River 69
mullet 105
Murphy, Gerry 124–5
Murrough *see* Sedge, great red

O

Octopus 131
Olive 18, 27, 33, 69, 147
O'Reilly, Peter 132
O'Shea, Neil 74–9
Owenea, River 134–5

PQ

Parson Tom 132
Pearson, Alan 132

Peirce, Roy 96, 99–101
  Sorcha 101
perch 99, 103
Peter Ross 26
Peters, Miles 140
pike 108–12, 153, 154
  fishing methods 113
pollock 104–5, 139
Powell, Ian and Glenda 56–60
prawning 61

R

rainbow trout 137, 140–41, 144–5
Rapala lure 51
Regan, Hi 66, 117
roach 99
Ruane, Judd 132
rudd 103

S

salmon 35, 36, 41
  fishing methods 83–5
  grilse 100, 119
  hatchery, Delphi 90–93
  prawning for 61
  spawning 156–7
  stocks 136–8
Samford, Chris 25
sea bass 78, 104–5
sea fishing 78, 104–5
sea trout 31–5, 36, 39–40, 42, 72–9, 88–90, 132–3
sedge 27, 33, 146, 147
  great red 27
  Welshman's button 147
Shannon, River 62
Sheelin, Lough 142–7
  fishing methods 147
Sheringham H.T. 25
Shiels, Basil 96–8

shrimp 50, 51, 99
Silver Badger 35
Silver Doctor 43
Silver Invicta 26
Silver Rat 35
Silver Stoat 35
sonaghan 128–31
Sooty Olive 26, 79
spooking fish, avoiding 94–5
Stoat's Tail 50, 51
Sullivan, Alan 39–41

TUV

tench 103–4
Thunder and Lightning 35
Toby lure 51
trolling 17, 51
trout
  brown 22, 33, 69, 100, 101, 146
  ferox 16, 17–18, 33, 100
  rainbow 137, 140–41, 144–5
  sea 31–5, 36, 39–40, 42, 72–9, 88–90, 132–3

WXYZ

Waterlog magazine 128
Waterville 72–4, 138
Watson's Fancy 79
Whelan, Ken 80–87, 136–41
Williams, Graham 120–27, 152–3, 155
Williams, Roy 132
Willy Gunn 50, 51
wrasse 104–5
Wulff patterns 124, 147
Yates, Christopher 11
A Year of Liberty, Walter Peard 88
zebra mussel 131–2

GREAT FISHING HOUSES OF IRELAND

For more information about the fishing houses mentioned in this book, please visit the websites given below.

Arrow Lodge:
www.arrowlodge.com

Ashford Castle:
www.ashford.ie

Ballynahinch Castle:
www.ballynahinch-castle.com

Butler Arms Hotel:
www.butlerarms.com

Delphi Lodge:
www.delphilodge.ie

Glencar House:
www.glencarhouse.com

Grasshopper Cottage:
www.troutfishingireland.com

Healy's Restaurant & Country House Hotel:
www.healyspontoon.com

Lough Inagh Lodge Hotel:
www.loughinaghlodgehotel.ie

Millbank House:
www.millbankhouse.com

Acknowledgements

"It is in the shelter of each other that the people live." Irish Proverb

Let me stress at once that this book would never have been remotely possible without the huge enthusiasm and generosity of many, many Irish people. I must start by mentioning Patrick O'Flaherty, at Ballynahinch Castle, both for his generosity when I stayed with him and for his help in setting up meetings in other great fishing houses in Ireland. Thank you so much, Patrick. Before leaving Ballynahinch, I also want to thank Mike Conneely, Alan Sullivan, and all the staff who proved so generous in their information and anecdotes.

At Ashford Castle, many, many thanks to Rory Murphy, Frank Costello, and Jimmy Foy. The whole Lough Arrow experience, whether for trout or pike, has been brought alive for me by the enthusiasm of Rob and Steph Maloney. I'd also like to thank Maire O'Connor for all her generosity during my stay at Inagh Lodge, and Colin Folan for his fascinating insights. At Glencar, many thanks indeed to Kevin, Vincent, and Michael.

Ian and Glenda Powell – what a great place you run down at Blackwater Lodge, and thank you so much for those days of help and entertainment. Can I also thank the Keays family for all their help on the Shannon and the Mulcair. Richard and Eleanor, I'll always be in your debt. Thank you, too, to Mick Doherty for revealing so many of the subtleties of small river fly fishing to me. I'd like to thank all at the Butler's Arms down in Waterville – what a tremendous base for an angling holiday – and especially one of the top guides there, Neil O'Shea.

Many, many thanks to you, Ken Whelan, for your continuing advice and generosity during my journeys over to the island. And thank you, too, for putting me in touch with James Pembroke, who has so many right ideas, as does Peter Mantle at Delphi. Thank you so much, Peter, for your help, and I wish you continuing success in all that you do. Back on Corrib, thank you to Basil Shiels and Roy and Sorcha Peirce for your time and knowledge so gladly shared. Basil, I will be after those ferox soon. Moving up to Conn, thank you John Dever, both for putting Healy's Hotel to rights and also for your bulldog determination to see the fishing back to what it once was. Graham Williams, Jerry Murphy, and Gordon Heath… thank you all three for making my trip such a delightful one. Jim Dillon, thank you so much for the excellent day I spent with you. Up on the Belle Isle Estate, in Northern Ireland, may I thank Charles Plunkett for his continuing help and generosity over the years. Can I also thank both Mike Shortt and Chris Meehan for the massive amount of effort they've both put into this book and for helping me as I've travelled the length and breadth of Ireland. Without you both it would have been difficult to have even started! And without the sterling services of Irish Ferries, who constantly proved so generous and accommodating, I would never even have got across the water! What an excellent service you provide these days. Above all, can I thank Richie Johnston, who has helped me on so many Irish projects over the years. Richie, I don't owe you one: I owe you a thousand.

I'd also like to thank Carol, Andrew, and Ian for your painstaking efforts over this book and for the huge amount of input you've all made. I also want to thank Deborah for her understanding and, last but not least, Shitabob for his calm acceptance of the Irish weather and the grandeur of Ashford Castle.